The Way to Write for Television

SERIES EDITORS JOHN FAIRFAX & JOHN MOAT

The Way to Write for Television

ERIC PAICE

Elm Tree Books • London

First published in Great Britain 1981
by Elm Tree Books/Hamish Hamilton Ltd
Garden House 57-59 Long Acre London WC2E 9JZ

Copyright © 1981 by Eric Paice

British Library Cataloguing in Publication Data

Paice, Eric
    The way to write for television.
    1. Fiction — Authorship
    I. Title

    ISBN 0 241 10650 8
    ISBN 0 241 10647 8 Pbk

Printed in Great Britain by
Redwood Burn Limited, Trowbridge, Wiltshire,
and bound by Pegasus Bookbinding, Melksham, Wiltshire.

Contents

Chapter One

> A man may write at any time, if he will set himself doggedly to it.
>
> Dr. Johnson

Television writing is scarcely thirty years old. Too young to be considered an art form, too loose and ephemeral for a mature body of considered criticism to have been established. Until the invention and mass availability of the video recorder, a television play or series would appear before a mass audience for a brief hour, then vanish like the morning dew. And the television companies were extraordinarily profligate with material that seemed to them to be in unending supply. Most of the plays produced in the late fifties and early sixties were wiped so that the tapes on which they were recorded could be used again. To find any trace of them today you must rummage in the attics of writers with storage space to keep their old scripts.

It was instant drama, with no shelf life.

Today, of course, a play can be preserved by anyone with a home recording device. It can be studied, broken down into its component parts and its bones laid bare. Since new writers have no access to studios (and even established writers are often kept at a distance), the recorder becomes a valuable training device.

But if television writing is not yet an art form at least it is a skilled craft, and like all crafts, can be learnt.

But I must start with a few words of warning.

Are you quite sure you *want* to write for television?

Well, of course you do. You are stuck in the endless tedium of an office, factory or behind the kitchen sink. You want to break out and express yourself. You want the *freedom* that a writer appears to enjoy. You may even be enticed by the money (though there is less of it than you might think). And above all you want the status — your name up on the screen with all the fame or notoriety that you believe that might entail. But pause a moment. Stop the first person you meet and ask how many television writers they can actually remember by name. Dennis Potter, perhaps. Even the late David Mercer. After that there will be a deadly hush. For the sad fact is that most writers for the box are virtually anonymous. Their names appear momentarily amongst a long and rapidly moving credits list amongst the producers, directors, wardrobe supervisors, lighting cameramen, make-up girls and production unit managers. Although you may be reaching an audience a hundred times greater in a single night than Shakespeare in his lifetime, perhaps (with world wide sales) vaster than the audience for every playwright strung end to end since the dawn of history, you will be less well known than a novelist writing his first book, or a stage dramatist playing to fifty people in an out-of-town fringe theatre.

You are the invisible factor in production. If the audience notices your wit or dramatic skill, they will recall only the actor who delivers your lines. If a newspaper critic detects your hand in the work at all, he is more likely to knock it than to praise it. Critics, on the whole, do not like writers — perhaps because they see them as extensions of themselves, and instinctively obey the laws of electro-magnetism — like poles repel.

And if, by some mischance, you are taken up by the critics as the newest white hope on the television horizon — beware. They will give you your moment in the sun, from thereon they will wait with almost mischievous pleasure for you to take a tumble.

Put not your faith in critics. Their job is to write bright copy — and in these days of iconoclastic journalism, bright copy is knocking copy.

So if fame is your spur, praise your unguent or literary stature your ambition, television writing is *not* for you.

Neither will you have the simple pleasure of seeing the audience enjoy (or otherwise react) to your work, as you can in the theatre. It is a cottage industry. For most of your life you will see nothing but the view from your study window, hear neither praise nor complaint from the passing crowds who do not even know who you are, though you have entered their sitting rooms, cajoled, harrassed or entreated them the night before.

Finally, if I may depress you even further, do not imagine that with your first play you have stepped on the bottom rung of a ladder that reaches up to greater things. Too often, in the lifetime of a television writer, the process tends to be reversed. Yesterday's sparkling bright playwright, finding he cannot live on the occasional income from single plays, turns his hand to the series. Here the degree of originality is less (unless it is his own series, and even then it is heavily proscribed by company demand). But it is on the series

2

that he will really start to learn the craft. He will also discover that although he is now using greater skills, judged by the aesthetic snobbery that prevails in the media, he has actually taken one step *down* the ladder. He is now in the world of entertainment, where more is deemed to be worse.

But at least he can afford the new house, the new car and possibly the new wife or husband. Then the taxman cometh, and to retain his new acquisitions, he finds he must now do a stint on the soap operas where the money is better because he can turn out more of them in a shorter time. Television writing is probably the only profession outside grave digging where you start at the top and end up at the bottom.

Unless, like the phoenix, you can rise again. But we shall come to that later on.

The old forms die hard, and none harder than the English academic tradition where critical faculties are rated above creative impulse, to write for the popular market is a betrayal of intellectual faculties; when even to admit owning a television set is considered rather vulgar.

How much more vulgar, then, to actually write for it?

But once you have accepted that this is the prevailing climate in which you have chosen to exercise your craft, can honestly swear on your heart that you are no longer troubled by it — more, that you are actually rather excited by it — then you are free to write for television.

And in doing so, you will find you have entered quite a different world. But it is not an either/or world. Quantity and quality are not sworn enemies. They lie side by side. Television is still all embracing enough to cater for all tastes, though how long it will continue to do so will depend largely on you, the writer.

Television? No good will come of this device. The word is half Greek, half Latin.

C. P. Scott

So what is television writing?

Half this? Half that? Or half the other?

Certainly it began as a hybrid form. When it first came on air, the only writers around with any dramatic experience came either from Sound Radio, Film, or the Theatre. Although it has since assumed an identity of its own, these three influences are still there in greater or lesser degree. The radio and theatrical influence was probably dominant in the sixties. It was then still principally a writers' medium. But from the early seventies on, the Director began to dominate the scene. There was a substantial shift towards filming on location as distinct from shooting with video cameras in studio. This was partly in pursuit of greater realism, partly because of continuing improvements in fast film stock and the ability to shoot in poor light, not least out of a general feeling of claustrophobia inside the studio complex. Writing styles changed with the new freedom of movement. Scripts became leaner, less wordy and more reliant on the mood and atmosphere of the location itself. And, of course, more action packed. Though this was not a necessary corollary of the move towards film, there are few directors who can resist an action sequence even when it is not strictly germane to the plot.

Then, for a short period, a peculiar form of hybrid journalism arrived as an importation from America. Some called it docu-drama, some fact/fiction (which soon became abbreviated to 'faction'). The classic example was *All The President's Men,* the searing tale of Watergate, blending recent history with what can best be described as dramatic licence. Britain was soon in the field with *Suez.* (The form was not, in fact, original, it had grown out of a theatrical device called the *Living Newspaper,* first invented by the Red Army, later developed by the US Federal Theatre project, then by London's Unity Theatre in the late thirties.) So now we were into a different combination — crossing journalism with stage tech-niques. But it proved only to be a passing fashion — history was getting much too close for comfort.

The BBC tried another cross. The dramatized documentary. Barely distinguishable from the 'faction' except that it was set safely in the past. *The Voyage of the Beagle* was told in this form, not by the Drama Department, but by the Documentary and Features Department. The form still continues, but is beginning to prove just as expensive as drama itself. It has now reached the point where it cannot be produced at all without a substantial injection of overseas money. But these experiments remain diversions from the mainstream. The bulk of television writing is still in the drama and comedy field and will remain so at least for the next decade.

4

Imagery and the confines of the imagination

ANTE OMNIA VERBUM

is the slogan emblazoned on the fragment of the Rosetta Stone that forms the crest of the Writers Guild of Great Britain.

and for those with small Latin and less Greek it means, roughly translated, 'In the beginning was the word'. But is it true?

In the strict sense that there can be no production without the script, it has a narrow, literal truth. In another sense it is misleading. In the very beginning — before the caveman discovered language — was the dream and the image. And television is essentially about images. Though that may seem obvious to the viewer, it is surprising how many beginner writers still treat it as though it was a literary form with illustrations added.

The film director John Boorman once described film making as money turned into light, then back again into money. In a similar equation, television writing might be considered as images turned into words, then back into images.

But the images come first. Without visual imagery, no words on a page can be rekindled into dramatic movement. Dramatic dialogue, of course, performs more functions that that, and we shall deal with this in a later chapter, but the essential framework in which it is contained must first be pictured in the mind's eye.

But imagery without constraint is chaos. The art of storytelling is getting your thoughts in order; giving them shape and form. Television is heavily structured and paradoxically, the visual dimension of the form itself imposes brutal limitations on the imagery the writer has created. Perhaps the best way to illustrate this point is to go back to one of the strands I mentioned as an early influence in the genesis of television drama — sound radio. One of the delights of writing for radio is that the audience itself provides the visual factor. You present them with the characters, their conflicts and the general ambience in which they are set. The listener provides the pictures in his or her own head. Television denies the audience that dimension by providing it for them. What you see has deprived you of imagining what might be there. The director has flooded the stage with light and form, defined both its geometry and its geography. In so doing he has denied the viewer the power to explore beyond those boundaries except as the confines of the set dictate. He has provided him with light, but denied him shadow, and so drained the tension out of the experience.

To take an extreme analogy, when you enter a darkened room particularly if you have never entered it before, you are full of

5

tension. Anything or anyone may be lurking in the darkness. The moment you switch on the light, all that tense expectation is lost. An encelograph reading of the brain would show a sudden nosedive back to normality. And if drama is about anything, it is about maintaining tension and suspense.

When I first started writing for the box in the late fifties, plays went out live and in black and white. I hated the introduction of colour with its intense candle power, just as I regarded taped recordings with the opportunities for endless retakes as more of a hindrance to drama than a help. Improved technology had taken away two essential dramatic ingredients, the sharp contrasts of light and shade and the tension between actors knowing that this was the one and only performance — a tension you could feel coming through the box, even sitting at home by your fireside.

Light, without shade, vitiates drama.

But there is no turning back the clock. On our television screens today we see all, hear all and one day may feel all. The art of the dramatist is to find ways of putting back the dramatic intensity the lighting men have taken away in order to accommodate the tyranny of colour intensity.

It is in the disciplining of the images in the mind so that they can be contained within the tightlaced limits of the means of production that the new writer finds the greatest difficulty. This problem, of course, is common to all creative processes, whether it is writing a novel, constructing a poem or painting a picture. But in television, the final process, the reconstitution of those images distilled into the script, is not in your hands — it is carried out by the director, the actors, the lighting cameraman and all the other people involved in production. The script must therefore be created in a language that they will all understand in common. Perhaps the nearest analogy is the work of an architect. He has first conceived the building in his head, now he must condense his thoughts into a detailed blue print that can be read by the quantity surveyor, the builder, carpenter, plasterer, painter and electrician. If the architect has got a fundamental detail wrong, the building may collapse. Plays can also collapse and many have done so. All of these production people must feel they can trust the writer to have got it right in the first place. That is one of the main reasons why television companies tend to use the same writers again and again, particularly in the series and serials. They feel they can trust them to get the plans right.

6

Chapter Two

I've got a marvellous idea for a play — and it's definitely original!

> Our principal writers have all been fortunate in escaping a regular education.
>
> Hugh McDiarmid

Ideas. Where do they come from?

Are they original — and does it matter?

On the very few occasions I have sat behind an editor's desk, I would often amuse myself by trying to identify the source of the 'new and original' ideas that came flooding in from both new and established writers. *Romeo and Juliet* was a steady favourite, usually from writers dealing with ethnic minorities — black boy, white girl, Catholic/Protestant, Jewish/Gentile, or various combinations thereof. The age gap problem play was usually a variation on the same theme. Curiously enough I don't ever recall seeing a plagiarized *Othello* amongst the ethnic problem plays, though I'm sure the Americans have done it to death. Many a modern thriller series owes its origins to *Macbeth*; *Coriolanus* crops up occasionally, usually in plays about tycoon businessmen where it's tough and lonely at the top, though *Hamlet* seems to be more popular with comedy writers than dramatists (indecisive anti-heroes with dotty girl friends and in-law problems). There's nothing wrong with plagiarizing Shakespeare, of course, and the Bard himself took most of his best plots from other people. Even well-known writers will plagiarize themselves from time to time. The critic Philip Purser once pointed out that Dennis Potter's banned play *Brimstone and Treacle* was actually a re-working of his earlier play *Job's Ark*. It is not uncommon for writers to stay with the same themes until they feel they have fully exploited their potential.

But since most television drama is contemporary realism, by far the most common story source is media feedback. Many a good play owes its origins to half a column in the morning newspapers. Later on in this book I shall be taking two such themes and showing the different ways in which they might be exploited. But inevitably, a fair amount of material is simply fed back from television itself, often very thinly disguised. Sometimes this is deliberate — a writer hoping to get away with it — but more often it is quite unconscious. An idea or theme, culled from the box, slips away into the author's subconscious mind then emerges a year later as a bright new thought. The new writer, when faced with the charge that he has lifted the plot from a previous programme, will invariably look amazed. He genuinely cannot remember having seen it before. He believes he has taken it from real life. And to a certain extent this is valid, for if most of his leisure time has been spent watching the box, television entertainment has *become* reality.

'Listen, in television film there's only one goddam plot. There's a guy in Zanzibar with a cork up his arse. There's only one guy in the world who can get it out and he lives in Newark, New Jersey. We spend the next fifty minutes seeing the second guy fighting overwhelming odds to reach the first guy before he dies of toxic poisoning. O.K.?'
Attributed to a U.S. Distributor — but probably invented by a writer.

As more and more television fiction saturates our lives, ideas, plots and formats become increasingly incestuous, until the bemused writer begins to ask himself, 'What *is* original?' Even, 'What is reality?' in a world of recurring mirror images.

More significantly, 'Do the buyers of television material really care whether it is or not?'

And the answer to the last question, surprising as it may seem, is that they not only care but are constantly in search of it. That is why they will, from time to time, turn to the new writer — the virgin mind.

They hope.

To return to the quotation from Hugh McDiarmid at the beginning of this section, he is, of course, quite right. You do not need a degree in English Literature to write for television, and if you have one it may even be to your disadvantage. Your critical faculties may have been developed to a point where they suppress the creative idea before it is even born.

Some of the best writing for television has come from people who left school in their mid-teens and spent their formative years in factories, down mineshafts, or serving in shops. The experiences they gained from direct contact with the kind of life the mass of their audience understand is their most valuable asset, and because it was obtained at their most impressionable age, it is deeply etched.

But where *television itself* has become a major constituent part of their education, the hypothesis turns full circle. There is no such thing as the virgin mind. We are all conditioned by a variety of influences — *not the least of which is television fiction.* Originality is largely a new way of arranging the pieces in the kaleidoscope and reality is in the eye of the beholder. The only thing that is unique is you. *Your* subjective viewpoint, *your* particular way of seeing reality, *your* capacity to observe human nature in your own way. And that is really all you need. It may not be all the buyers of television material ask of you, but it is all you should be prepared to offer them.

> Better to write for yourself and have no public, than to write for the public and have no self.
>
> Cyril Connolly

Groundplans, bricks and mortar . . .

The concept.

You wake in the morning, head buzzing with ideas. How do you select the one that's going to flower? They all seem equally exciting at this stage — and this time in the morning.

You've worried at the ideas all day, and by the evening, they all seem dull and uninspired.
So what has gone wrong?
The first thing is that you have probably worried most of them to death and are now exhausted, not so much with the ideas as with the worry.
So the next lesson to learn is never to try to evaluate ideas when

9

you are tired. Forget them. Think of something else. Read a book, listen to some music, take the dog for a walk — anything. If any one of those ideas is really any good, it will come back of its own accord. And when it does, *write it down*. And write it in whatever form it first came into your mind. If it was posed as a question, write it down as a question. If as a revelation of truth about the world, or an epigram, or a prophecy, put it down exactly as it was conceived. It may have occurred to you as an exchange of dialogue — if so, you have a head start because the idea is going to end up as dialogue in any case. Don't try to change it from its original form by literalizing it or clothing it in different language. This is the image. The seed. You can easily destroy it. Since we can't discuss ideas in a vacuum, let me pose one for you. A one word idea . . .

TRAPPED

and see what it conjures up. A physical trap? Not much mileage in that. It could be a hunter caught in a bear trap, but that's just a variation on our Zanzibar friend. People trapped in a fire? That was done in *Towering Inferno*. Besides the options are pretty simple. They either get rescued or burnt to death. Back to Zanzibar, and expensive to shoot. So try a psychological trap. This has the immediate advantage that it is about relationships between people. Actors are cheaper than burning buildings and give better value. It can be done in studio and will probably gain in atmosphere for being confined in a small space. Producers are going to like that, it keeps the budget down.

Now someone is trapping someone, but using no physical force. By what means? Exploitation of a sense of duty? Guilt? Probably a mixture of both, we shall see. A grown up daughter trapped by her sense of duty into looking after her ailing parents? That was done several years ago in a novel called *A Dutiful Daughter* by the Australian author Thomas Keneally. It is also a variation on the *King Lear* plot — or could be if you regard Cordelia as the victim rather than the old man himself. And why not? Immediately that thought occurs you are, consciously or unconsciously employing a device employed by all professionals when they are thinking around a subject — *role reversal*. Take the observed relationship and turn it on its head so that victor becomes victim. Are the parents using the daughter's sense of duty to blackmail her, or is the relationship more subtle than that? Could the daughter be trapping the parents by making *them* feel guilty — perhaps as revenge for an imagined (or real) injury to her personality in childhood. Something to do with sibling rivalry and the preferential treatment towards one child rather than another. Now we have a sister or a brother. The stage is beginning to fill with people. We have the beginnings of a play.

We could have taken a different relationship. A more everyday theme. Husband and wife trapped in a hopeless marriage. With divorce on tap it may seem a rather looser trap than it might have been twenty years ago — unless they are practising Catholics, or Hindus living in Ruislip (an ethnic minority spin-off from the original idea — but unless you are an Indian living in Ruislip, you might be better to steer clear of that one). On the other hand, a sense of duty doesn't end with the divorce courts. Many people take it with them into the second marriage — particularly when there are children involved. Now you are peopling the stage again. You have the beginnings of a play on second marriages.

Or there may be no family relationship at all. Go back into history to Sinbad the sailor — he helped the old man across the river, then found he could not get him off his back. A little research will reveal that this was based on an ancient Chinese law that made a man responsible for another if he saved him from drowning, since he had now taken on the role of God.

But you are already starting to wander, and not to any good purpose since Beckett has already dealt with that in *Waiting for Godot*. On the other hand, the exercise has been useful. It has shown you the universality of the subject. It may also have led you towards the obverse of the original key word that started off your train of thought. If most of us are trapped in some way or other by behaviour patterns or problems of our own devising, what is freedom? Does it even exist? According to the Marxist dictum, freedom is the knowledge of necessity. But now you are off into a different play.

So that single word 'trapped' has already acted as a trigger for a wide range of creative thinking. But supposing you had chosen a word that sounds as though it might have the same meaning — 'caught'. Would that have led to the same creative excursions? In fact it wouldn't. It is not such a powerful word. It is static, containing no movement. Frozen in time. The experienced playwright would know that instinctively and wouldn't bother to waste his time on it.

This has simply been an exercise to show how a single word can trigger off ideas, but before anyone starts sitting down to write plays on a 'trapped' theme I have to confess it has already been done. It was the generic name for a play anthology I edited for ATV in the sixties.

Though there is nothing to stop anyone trying it again from a different angle.

A line of dialogue may also trigger off a play idea. Perhaps the classic example was a play by Terence Frisby called *And Some Have Greatness Thrust Upon Them*. The idea for this play arose from a chance line he overheard from a pregnant girl: 'My friend Sylvie said it was safe standing up.'

11

The BBC accepted the play, then got cold feet (censorship was tougher in those days, even though Mrs Whitehouse had not yet appeared on the scene) and edited the original line out. Frisby protested and finally took the BBC to court on the grounds that the line was the essential structure on which the play was compounded. He won the case, but relationships had become so soured that he never worked for the BBC again. Instead he gave his next play, *A Girl in My Soup,* to a theatre management. That single line trigger for a play set him off on a course which made him a small fortune.

Chapter Three

The Premise

'And remember drama takes place *in time*, and the dramatic moment is whenever a change, a turning point takes place. It's when a character discovers something which makes him act differently. It's where a story is moving in one direction, something happens and it starts moving in another direction. If you can keep in mind the turning points in the narrative, the moments of change, you are safe. That is the most golden advice I can give.'

Sydney Newman, Producer of ABC's Armchair Theatre and one-time Head of BBC Drama.

Sydney Newman's advice on this occasion was delivered to his young producers at BBC Television Centre in 1966. But it could equally have been made to writers today.

For many years, the standard work on play construction was *The Art of Dramatic Writing* by a Hungarian American, Lajos Egri. There have been a number of books written since then on the subject, but most draw some inspiration from Egri's work.

He maintained that the plot of any play or film could be reduced to one brief statement which he called *The Premise:* by dictionary definition, a proposition stated or assumed as leading to a conclusion.

Ibsen's *A Doll's House,* for example, can be reduced to the simple premise: A wife, treated as a toy, will revolt as a human being. The premise of *Macbeth* would be: Ruthless ambition drives people to their own destruction. Or of *Othello:* Jealousy so consumes a man that he destroys the one he loves. It is, of course, relatively simple to summarize a play in these terms *after* it is written and, if used indiscriminately, can lead to different interpretations. Thus the premise of Little Red Riding Hood could be: Wolves should make sure there are no woodcutters around before they dress up in drag. Or equally: Little girls should have their eyes tested before visiting their grandmothers.

But the function of the premise is not simply to define the moral of the story, it is to give the author a simple instruction about the *purpose* of his plot. All the premises prepared by Egri contain the seeds for developing the story from a proposition to a conclusion. In other words, they embrace *change* during the course of the narrative itself. By this measure, both premises I provided for Little Red Riding Hood cannot be considered valid since they imply action before the story begins. Indeed, had either the wolf or Ms Hood taken these precautions there would have been no story at all. So perhaps the first thing to learn about the use of the premise is how to construct the premise itself. It must contain forward movement.

Sydney Newman is saying the same thing. He advises his producers to look for those points in a play where change takes place, the story, moving in one direction, then starts to move in another. He defines this as the moment when the character discovers something which makes him behave differently. Most probably, the character will have discovered something about himself. And that 'something' must be contained in the premise, the original concept. If it is not there in the beginning, you cannot put it in halfway through. The potential for change must be in the seed.

It would be misleading to suggest that all professional writers work in this rather mechanistic way. Plays are often created empirically, without the author necessarily knowing where he is going from the outset. In fact, this is one of the pleasures of dramatic writing, to discover new facts of your characters as you go along. But that is a game for tightrope walkers, who rely on their own subconscious instincts to keep the story under control. Most of the good professional dramatists *are* tightrope walkers, but they had to learn how to keep their balance first of all.

You have to know the rules before you can afford the confidence to break them.

So far we have touched on two ways of organizing your thoughts in order to make a story possible. The exploitation of the single, evocative word like 'trapped' and the construction of the premise. But there is a long way to go yet.

At the Arvon Foundation, my co-tutor Fay Weldon and I used a key 'trigger' word to set the sixteen students in motion. We used the word 'departure', asking them to conceive a situation, or recall it from their own experience, where people were parting from each other, and as a consequence of that parting, their lives were changed.

14

But there was no imperative for change on both parties — either the person leaving, or those left behind. That was for the students to determine. They might even determine that despite the prospect of change, there had, in fact been no change at all. All these options were open. Then, just to make things difficult, we insisted that they must conceive this situation *outside their own age group*. For example: 'You are sixteen years old and leaving home for the first time.'

Since some of the students were middle-aged, this was a rather demanding condition, but we knew that most people would automatically think of themselves as they are now, acting and reacting in the maturity of experience unless we made this provision.

We wanted them to re-create themselves as they had been, or as they *believed* they had been, together with the people around them at that time. In essence, we were asking them to recreate a moment from their youth.

It was an extraordinarily difficult task to set, demanding total honesty. And they responded in a quite extraordinary way. Within forty-eight hours, some were in tears, finding that through their own writing they had opened up all kinds of painful experiences and discovered things about themselves they had not, until that moment realized.

Others reacted quite differently. One man in his fifties — now a Devon hotelier — evoked a remarkably vivid picture of his own adolescence, full of hope, confidence and the sheer exhilaration of his youth in the North East. He discovered he had almost total recall of those years, and because they excited him, the scenes he wrote enthralled the other students when he read it out to them. They did so because he had been able to step outside himself, free from all the worries, fears and conditioned reflexes of his present existence. He had found the freedom to create characters, characters he knew well, but could now observe from sufficient distance to preserve in balance. Although the central character was himself, it was both a different self and his own self. He had overcome the first vital hurdle — the playwright's ability to live both inside and outside the character he has created.

Character creating . . .

Every writer is a thief — he steals from other people's lives.
Camus

Books on writing convey the impression, at least tacitly, that anyone can become a writer. That may or may not be so as far as other forms of writing are concerned, but if I have given the impression so far that just anyone can become a dramatist so long as they follow certain rules, then I must hasten to correct it. There are some people who will never be able to write drama (or comedy for that matter) without undergoing a total personality change.

The reason is painfully simple. They are thick.

More elegantly phrased, they lack sensitivity. This does not make them less lovable, or kind, or even less clever. You will find insensitive people in every walk of life, from dustmen to diplomats, plumbers to politicians, schoolmasters to saggermaker's bottom knockers. And you are just as likely to find them in the television industry as anywhere else. Odd as it may seem, you are more likely to find sensitivity and perception amongst Chief Constables than you are amongst Senior Executives of television stations. The reason is not hard to find, the cop has spent a lifetime with his eyes and ears open and his mental antennae finely tuned, while the Managing Director of Albion Television may have needed little more than a flair for accountancy or a relentless capacity for hard work to reach his position. And more often than not, a blind eye and a deaf ear. Like the cop, the dramatist not only has to keep his eyes and ears open, he also has to be a judge of character, and the best way to judge character is to have formed the habit of observing it — preferably from childhood. In any group of children in a playground, it is not difficult to pick the one who is most likely to make it as a dramatist. He (or she) will be the one on the edge, close enough to listen and watch, but not so close as to be distracted from this entertaining pursuit by involvement in the activity itself. When he goes to bed that night he will most probably be replaying the events in his head, re-arranging the people involved, examining their motives, working out his own imaginary responses to each turn of event as though he had actually been involved in the action. This makes him sound like the traditional nasty little swot, but far from it. He is probably not doing terribly well in his lessons, since he has already discovered that human behaviour is far more interesting than dry facts. His teachers are beginning to despair of him anyway, he spends too much time watching *them* instead of the blackboard. He is also showing a dangerous tendency towards lateral thinking — coming in at a subject sideways or at a dozen different angles instead of head on.

But he will survive because he has learnt, from his close study of people, how to manipulate them.

And how to steal.

16

Nothing of substance, just bits of dialogue here, aspects of behaviour there, odd quirks of nature and the facial expressions that accompany a thought. Later on he will steal entire characters and store them away for his own use. He is a magpie.

But collecting characters is one thing, setting them in motion quite another. To do that he will have to learn to orchestrate. The problem with creating characters is that once you have done so, and placed them inside your mental stage, you can't just leave them around sulking in corners. They have to justify their reason for being there. Even if a character has very little to say, he will affect the other characters merely by his presence. One of the commonest faults of the new writer is to create a character for a particular line or function in a scene, then promptly forget all about him. Remember that some poor actor has to play that part and if you don't give him or her something to do they will be sorely tempted to do things you never intended. And that can ruin your scene.

Creating characters is really quite an awful responsibility. You have opted to play God, and must assume His burdens. You too will have to know when a single sparrow falls, so don't create any form of life on the stage, even sparrows, unless you are prepared to look after them.

There is a rather ugly word used in the business called 'telescoping'. This is really a euphemism for culling the characters and dialogue you don't actually need, and so tightening up the script. To take a common, everyday example: A man walks into a restaurant to keep a lunch appointment with his wife/mistress/ client/lover. He asks the waiter for the menu, orders his food then gives his wine order to the wine waiter. He then gets on with the business for which he came. You have set the scene in your head. You know just such a restaurant and have a mental image of each character involved. You have also just used up three speaking parts before you've even started the scene. Immediately you can telescope the two waiters into one by asking the table waiter to give your wine order to the wine waiter — the viewer is quite happy to accept that this will be done off camera. By telescoping two waiters into one you have just taken about a hundred pounds off the budget and lost nothing. Now try disposing of the other waiter. 'Ah,' you may object, 'I need that waiter to establish, by his familiarity with my principal character that he is a regular, on his home ground, so putting the wife/mistress/client/lover at ease (or at a disadvantage, depending on the purpose of the scene).' That is a valid point and a useful device to give the right edge to the scene that follows. But are you sure it can't be done by a line from the principal character himself — or from his dining partner? Even by the confidence with which he strides towards his familiar table in the corner?

The purpose of this illustration is not to encourage you to write restaurant scenes without waiters, merely to show that minor characters are not always as necessary as you think. A good actor, with the right line or gesture, can convey a whole host of information — providing you have made it clear to him what you wish to convey.

That, in its simplest form is what is meant by telescoping. If you go through the other scenes you are setting up in your head you will find several other places where you have created characters you don't really need.

But to return to the characters you *do* need, who are they and how much do you know about them?

The traditional advice given to writers when first learning the craft is that they must know everything about the principal characters — age, height, weight, emotional make-up, background, schooling, hobbies and pastimes. They must feel that they have grown up with these characters and can accurately predict how they will inspire or react to any twist and turn of the plot. American writing schools are particularly strong on this point. The dictum has its roots in the 'Method' school of acting, which in turn drew its inspiration from the Russian post-revolutionary acting style of Stanislavsky. But ironically, when these intensely researched characters appear on screen they are the same flat, two dimensional stereotypes that have appeard in a thousand other pieces of drama for the past twenty years. British writers tend to be more haphazard in their character research, concentrating mainly on emotional make-up, and to a certain extent physical appearance, but not worrying too much about the rest. Yet it is to Britain that the Americans are now turning to find television drama and comedy with fresh and original characterization.

Granted, the advice given by the American writing schools may be largely wishful thinking, since the production line process of American television tends to iron out all unique characteristics that may have appeared in the original script. But even allowing for the fact that the American writers may be thwarted by their producers from practising what they preach, I think there are dangers in the approach itself. You certainly need to be sufficiently familiar with your characters to motivate their behaviour and understand their reactions, but this elaborate *curriculum vitae* approach can often defeat its own purpose. By codifying your characters you can easily stereotype them, so predicating their responses that they have no space in which to grow, expand or even change their minds. The characters become trapped in their own moulds. Familiarity can breed contempt, or at least insensitivity. This is as true in the relationship between an author and his characters as it is between

18

partners in an indifferent marriage. Let your characters maintain their capacity to surprise you. Share with the viewer a certain mystery about them as new facets of their identity unfold.

Creating a play is an organic process, not a mechanical process.

By the time you have written the play you will know those characters completely and feel they are part of your life.

You then have the problem of getting rid of them so that you can get on with the next play. That is not as easy as it may sound. Some characters, if you have realized them vividly, have an irritating tendency to hang around in the mind, stubbornly refusing to be evicted. They can very easily influence the next group of characters you create. They are like lodgers who have still not left the premises. You will find them in dark corners of your mind, whispering away at the new tenants, influencing their behaviour and advising them how to handle the landlord to best advantage. What they are really doing, of course, is seeking immortality through their heirs. If they succeed, you will soon become known as a writer with only a limited range of characters at your disposal. That may not necessarily be to your disadvantage, many famous writers have made a fortune by using the same central character over and over again, but beware the trap.

Ordinary or extraordinary?

How big should my characters be — larger than life or merely typical of the common man? This question is often asked by new writers and it is a difficult one to answer. There is an old adage that screenwriting falls into two categories — extraordinary people in ordinary circumstances, or ordinary people in extraordinary circumstances. Many critics of television would say that it suffers from far too many ordinary people in ordinary situations.

We have been living in an age of Realism in television drama for some two decades now and a lot of people are complaining that it is time we all moved on to a new phase. Certainly the steady increase in the number of documentary and reality/feature programmes has been cutting the ground from under the dramatist's feet. But it is not really as simple as that. If you watch a re-run of plays like *Up the Junction* or *Poor Cow* — both considered to be the height of documentary realism in their time — they now seem rather force-fed, even romantic. The BBC series *Z Cars* seems distinctly unreal today in comparison with, say G. F. Newman's *Law and Order*. Perhaps in ten years' time, *Law and Order* will seem like a quaint flight of fancy. Lord Willis, creator of the much maligned (by the critics, not by the audience) *Dixon of Dock Green* has a batch of press cuttings from the fifties describing the programme as 'stark realism'. As indeed it was, in the popular concept of realism in those days.

Realism is not a static condition. It is merely what is perceived as realism at any one time.

But neither is it a continuing process of uncovering truth — like peeling the skins off an onion. You can only assume that if you first presume that realism and truth are the same thing, and there is an ultimate truth to be aimed at. But contemporary realism, by definition, can never be more than a single aspect — a camera angle on a corner of life that has largely been ignored until now. It is nimble footed. The moment you think you have captured it, that moment has passed.

> Now *here* you see, it takes all the running *you* can do, to keep in the same place. If you want to get somewhere else, you must run at least twice as fast as that!
> Lewis Carroll — *Through the Looking Glass*

Sydney Newman, the Canadian who probably did more for British television drama than anyone in its short history, had no illusions about holding a mirror up to nature. He used to describe his anthology of *Armchair Theatre* plays as *heightened realism,* recognizing the degree of artifice involved and the need to make the central character of any play that much larger than reality. It is not a bad target for the new writer to aim at. Generally speaking it is better to over-write a central character than to under-write it. A strongly drawn character can always be taken down in production if it appears to be going over the top. An under-written character may never survive the production process.

But however you draw the character, it will not stand up on its own. It will need to be in *conflict.*

this compliment to their powers of judgement, some thought the playwright was either being lazy or wasn't very good at his job.

In fact, these playwrights were in very good company. It would be a rash critic who could claim that all the questions posed in Hamlet were resolved — despite the litter of bodies around the stage. Tom Stoppard proved that at least one strand was capable of extension in *Rosencrantz and Guildernstern Are Dead*. Tidy endings came principally into vogue between the eighteenth and the first half of the twentieth centuries — significantly, alongside structured mathematics.

But the opportunities for experimenting with the open ended play are now more limited. The television networks are now engaged in their own form of conflict — the battle for the ratings — and are reluctant to risk losing audiences that have already shown marked signs of dwindling. So the well tailored play is back in fashion. Whether the new 4th Channel will encourage experimental forms remains to be seen, but for the moment, the soundest advice I can give to the new writer who wants to sell to the main channels is to stay with the traditional equation.

In defining the two elements of conflict as statement and counter-statement, it may first be necessary to explain what I mean by the word 'statement'. This should not be taken in its strictly literal sense as an embodiment in words of opinion or fact. It is the *presentation* of the proposition in a dramatic form. This may employ few words or none at all. In a Western, a posse riding out to hunt down an outlaw is a statement, yet perhaps not a word has been spoken. A woman getting up in the morning, packing her suitcase and taking away her personal belongings from the marital home is a statement — that she is leaving her husband. In this instance, his attempts to persuade her to come back might be the counter-statement. Alternatively, the counter-statement may be delayed — her realization that the alternative life she has chosen is no more satisfying than the one she has left. In this case the resolution may be her decision to return, but under new conditions or circumstances. Alternatively, the principal conflict may take place in the husband's reactions. Where there are two people involved, there are always at least two ways of telling the story.

But conflict should not be confused with mere argument or abrasiveness. Two people shouting at each other may simulate the appearance of conflict but it is not true conflict. Real conflict must involve a determination of will. At one level, Edward Albee's *Who's Afraid of Virginia Woolf?* may be seen as nothing more than a biting domestic quarrel, but there is, in fact, a determined clash of two strong wills, with both protagonists coming very close to destroying each other. It might be compared to a death struggle between two

22

stags clashing antlers — not an unlikely parallel since Albee is said to have originally conceived it as a battle between two homosexuals.

The following is an example of two separate ways of handling conflict, both of which are equally valid. The story is taken from life — a tragic event that became world headlines:

> In December 1980, John Lennon was shot outside his apartment block by an assassin who is said to have believed himself the *real* John Lennon, and his victim an imposter.

According to Press reports at the time, Lennon was totally unaware that the man who had been standing outside for three days in succession was there to murder him. He assumed him to be one of the many fans who traditionally worship at his domestic shrine. That may have been so, but Lennon was perfectly well aware that he could be killed at any time. As it happens I was in New York that night and the following morning, by chance, travelled in a hire car driven by the chauffeur whom Lennon used to take his son Sean to school every day. According to the chauffeur he had driven Lennon all over Long Island some weeks prior, looking for a house to live in where he could feel secure, but had failed to find one.

At about the same time, his future assassin must have been making preparations for his mission, obtaining the murder weapon, saving up for the air ticket and making the final adjustments to his personality that would persuade him that he, the assassin, was in fact Lennon, and the real John Lennon a poseur who must be eliminated.

The events, as they stand, have all the elements of high drama. The two protagonists, preparing for their fatal meeting, the one intent on murder; the other, although innocent of the device by which he would meet his death, aware that it could happen because of the unique envy that his fame engendered. Yet calmly carrying on with his daily routine at the recording studios.

The physical conflict, when it comes, lasts only a matter of seconds, but was already implicit from the outset. The resolution is the death of one, the imprisonment of the other and a shock of shame and guilt that hit the city in the hours after the murder and reverberated around the world.

That is one way of recounting the drama; a straight down the line re-enactment of the build-up to the event, the event itself and its repercussions.

But there is another way of treating the same event that is far more intriguing from the dramatist's viewpoint (indeed, the first way of telling the story scarcely needs dramatizing at all since it tells itself). That is to take it from the angle of the poseur-turned-killer.

23

At first sight it looks like the traditional Jekyll and Hyde story in modern dress, but in fact it is more terrifying than that. It is closest to the Teutonic legend of the *Döppelganger* — the belief that a man could have a counterpart exactly like himself, and must destroy it before it destroys him. In this treatment it is the assassin who becomes the central character, and the essential conflict is in the assassin's own mind. The victim, however famous, then becomes a secondary role.

It is now possible to take that story and transpose it to another setting if the writer wishes to do so. In fact it is a popular theme amongst science fiction writers — the transposition of one body into that of another.

No doubt, when the legal procedures are over, the killing of John Lennon will be reconstructed in dramatic form by someone — probably half-a-dozen people will attempt it, since it contains all the basic elements of a tragedy together with the frightening elements of paranoid schizophrenia taken to its final stage.

It also poses a further, and more general question which could equally relate to the assassination of Lincoln, Kennedy or Martin Luther King. In a society where a murderer can become as famous as his victim, who dares to afford himself the luxury of fame? That is a theme in itself.

But there is one reason why many dramatists, however skilled, would *not* attempt the John Lennon story, however apparent the conflict. To do so with any integrity they would have to be fully conversant with the dialogue it would entail. Lennon was unique in his use of verbal imagery, it would be a brave playwright who would attempt to re-create it.

Chapter Five

Give us the words and we'll finish the job . . .

Dialogue is the rock on which many a writer founders. You either have an ear for it or you don't. Conversely, there are many television playwrights of repute who have a superb ear for dialogue but a very uncertain hand at structuring plot. Quite often, plot and dialogue are working against one another. Dialogue is the means through which the plot is moved forward and it quite often refuses to lend itself to that function. It has other functions as well. It must define character, provide atmosphere and create tension. And it must do so in the most economical way. That is an awful lot of weight for mere words to carry.

> 'Good morning, George.'
> 'Good morning, Hilda.'
> 'How are you today?'
> 'I'm fine, Hilda, and yourself?'
> 'Not so bad, George, considering the lousy weather . . .'
> > drivel drivel, drivel drivel . . .

Any producer who finds a script on his desk with that opening isn't likely to read much further. Even if there are three rapes, four murders and an earthquake in the ensuing pages, he'll never know about them because he isn't likely to get that far.
Try again.

> 'Hullo George. Fit?'
> 'I'm not George, I'm Samantha and I feel terrific.'

At least he'll now read on to page two, if only to sort out his casting problems.

Yet the writer of the first example has done everything he was told. He has conveyed the following information to the viewer:

> That it is morning.
> That one character is called George.
> That the other character is called Hilda.

25

That they have both arrived on the scene feeling reasonably healthy.

That the weather outside is rotten.

Five bits of essential information in five lines, he feels, can't be a bad start. So where has he gone wrong?

In the first place he can't count. He has actually conveyed *six* pieces of information to the viewer. The sixth, and the crucial item as far as the viewer is concerned, is that these two people are *boring*, and are likely to become more so on further acquaintance. He might give them another half a dozen lines to confirm this opinion, then switch channels.

Secondly, he has already fallen into the bad habit of naming his characters, not once, but four times. He is trying to establish their identity for the audience, but the audience really couldn't care less if they have no names at all. The viewer is watching them for performance, and in the hope that they are about to do something interesting. They could be called Pinky and Perky for all the difference it makes at this stage.

The writer may protest that he had *intended* to create a feeling of banality. These are banal people, and this opening snatch of conversation is exactly the kind of verbal exchange you may hear in any home up and down the country. Because it is accurately observed, it must therefore be real. Later on in the narrative he intended to bring another character into the scene who would shake them out of their complacency and so change their lives. This approach has a sound pedigree. Harold Pinter is a master of the art. But he is a master of several other vital skills as well; the superbly constructed monologue, for example, where the surface banality of the character is suddenly torn apart to reveal the incoherent coherence of his innermost thoughts. And above all, since he started life as an actor, he is a master of writing meaning into pauses.

Roger Graef, the American director who brought a new dimension to British television by his 'fly on the wall' approach to reality, emphasized the failure of human beings to communicate except through hesitancy, incoherence and fragmented banalities, called it 'the space between words'. Every actor knows about the technique, it is part of his art to act in the pauses, and the best actors will scan the script avidly to search out these pauses, to find new ways of making the most ordinary remark seem significant by creating space around it.

Mike Leigh, who 'wrote', directed and produced *Abigail's Party,* first for the stage and later for television with enormous success, goes one step further. He works from improvisations; getting the cast together, introducing the theme, then leaving them to orchestrate it into words. What he is in fact doing is staging a creative process that the writer has normally improvised in his own head. But because the artistes are contributing the products of their own imagination, and reacting in characters they have discovered for themselves, they will give performances that are totally in tune. But controlling a live improvisation in such a way that you do not *appear* to be giving it a direction, is a very specialized skill. It also demands a carefully handpicked cast. This is what Dorothea Alexander, (who taught me the technique of improvisation at the City Literary Institute in the early fifties and remains one of the best practitioners of the art in this country today), calls 'creative playmaking'.

But it is a dangerous game for the inexpert. A similar attempt by another producer to create improvised drama on the box a few weeks after the transmission of *Abigail's Party* was a disaster.

Presenting the uncontrived banality of everyday speech is itself a contrivance, demanding great skill and a director who knows exactly what you are trying to achieve. Such directors are not thick on the ground.

The second attempt at creating opening lines similarly conveys information. But it also poses two questions in the audience's mind. Is Hilda desperately shortsighted, or has George had a sex change? At least it could be worth sticking around for a while to find out, and one trick the writer will employ to make sure that moment is delayed is to leave those two questions hanging in the air.

The next two lines may appear totally unconnected:

HILDA: I haven't seen the cat this morning.
SAMANTHA: It's in the dustbin. I wrang its neck.

And the two lines that follow will establish that there was nothing really wrong with Hilda's eyesight: Samantha (née George) has indeed undergone a personality change.

HILDA: But you always loved that cat.
SAMANTHA: I thought I loved it. Now I know it always disgusted me. It was a Tom. A filthy, lecherous, prowling sex maniac. It deserved all it got.

We have now established a source of conflict, but so far, no forward movement. But in the light of what has gone before, that is now easily remedied.

HILDA: George . . .
SAMANTHA: Samantha.
HILDA: I can't live with a cat slayer. I'm going to leave you
           . . .

27

She won't, of course, or there would be no story.

But a few pages later, you discover there isn't really a story anyway. You have now fallen into the opposite trap. In an attempt to get off to a nice bright start you have allowed your penchant for smart dialogue to distort your original intention. What you might initially have intended to write was a straightforward, poignant story of two people who had reached a decision that they could no longer live together. But the dialogue has taken over and led you by the nose towards a black comedy.

In the exercise we set to the Arvon Foundation students (referred to on page 14), I mentioned some of the remarkable results some of these students produced and the effect it had upon them. But there were other reactions, particularly when we tried a similar experiment the following year. Quite a number of people re-created scenes from their early lives in terms of comedy. Some of it was very funny but in most cases they had turned to comedy to *avoid* the expression of emotions they found difficult, or too painful to handle. Several of the students desperately resisted this interpretation of their work, but the more forcibly they argued the case, the more we knew it to be true. They had fallen back on the English tradition for handling emotional crises — you must laugh at them to stop them hurting.

It would be quite unfair to suggest that all comedy writers are simply avoiding the emotional expression that drama demands. Comedy writing is a highly-skilled craft, and comedy dialogue is, on the whole, much more difficult to construct than drama dialogue. Timing is often far more crucial. The best comedy writers do, in fact, handle emotions with consummate skill. Carla Lane's comedy series *Butterflies* is probably the best example of a superb blend of comedy underlined by tragedy in the Chekovian tradition. She claims that all her stories are basically sad stories. Traditionally, through the ages, comedy and tragedy have been inextricably linked, and Carla Lane has virtually changed the whole direction of the television situation comedy by returning to that tradition.

Nevertheless, burying deeply felt emotions behind the facade of a joke *is* a national characteristic and writers should be aware when they are doing it, *why* they are doing it.

Defining character through dialogue

There is a simple test which anyone can apply. Put a ruler down the left hand margin of any script so that it covers up the names of characters, then see if you can recognize which characters are speaking *from the dialogue alone*. Obviously the writer himself will be able to, since he wrote them, but try it on a friend. You may be surprised how difficult it is to identify them.

The hallmark of really good dialogue is that each character will have a distinct speech rhythm, together with certain idiosyncracies of expression that make it recognizable from the rest. Can you even recognize whether the character is male or female?

If they all sound alike then the writer has failed either to visualize the character clearly enough in the first place or retained it as a live character in his mind. The characters have either picked up each other's speech patterns, or worse still, all speak with the author's speech patterns.

> 'Yes, we *know* the line, but who says it?'
> 'Well it must be *you* ducky, *she* spoke last.'
>   Irate exchange between actor and director,
>   overheard at a rehearsal of a popular BBC serial.

In a serial of mine which is now, mercifully, only a bitter memory, I had asked for a meeting between the Head of Department, the Producer and myself to complain about substantial changes being made without my approval to the characters I had created. The Producer maintained that he did not like the principal female role. She was not his idea of what a career woman should be, he had therefore given leave to his editor to change her to the image he had in his own mind. I insisted that it was *my* character, not his, and that even if I wished to bow to his judgement, I still had no idea just what kind of a woman he *did* have in his mind. After a while he suddenly sprang to his feet and said, 'I know what we want. It's the woman in *Alien.*' The Head of Department snapped his fingers. 'That's it!' he said. 'That's exactly the character we're looking for — the woman in *Alien.*'

Since I had not seen *Alien* at the time, I called a friend when I got home who watches all the sci-fi films. He was equally puzzled. 'Are you sure they're not talking about the film of *Star Trek?*' he said. I checked back. They were. 'What,' I asked my friend, 'are this lady's particular characteristics?' 'She's completely bald,' he said. 'And incidentally, the part was originally written for a man. They cast a woman without changing a word of dialogue.' I walked off the series and left them to it. It died after thirteen weeks. *The responsibility for characterization in dialogue is yours, and yours only. You may have to fight hard to retain it and you may well lose that fight, but since your reputation as a writer may stand or fall on the quality of your dialogue, it is not a fight you can afford to lose too often.*

A few hints . . . and a few traps . . .

The hardest parts of any scene are the opening and closing lines. The middle tends to write itself. To some extent, the opening line of any new scene (after the first) will be determined by the closing lines of the previous scene. There are three terms in current use with which you need to be familiar:

> The tag
> The hook
> and the segue (usually pronounced *segui,* though not to be confused with the seguidilla, which is Spanish verse set to music).

The tag is quite simply the last line of a scene. It can have one of three functions (and if you are *very* clever it might serve all three simultaneously). It can be the line that sums up the contents of the scene; it can be the line that marks a turn or twist in the plot — or reveals a new aspect of character; or it can be a simple signpost that points to the content or location of the scene that is to follow.

The hook need not be a line at all. It can be a piece of action or a single shot. It is used mainly in thrillers, but not exclusively so. The word accurately describes its function. It is used to hook the viewer. On commercial television, where there are commercial breaks, it is used at the end of an act. It is, if you like, a double strength tag. In American series (and Australian, which are a poor relation) it is usually accompanied by half a bar of loud, discordant music known as 'the sting'. In Britain we don't underscore so heavily.

The segue is a term used more by directors than by writers. It is quite simply a link. It may be a piece of linking dialogue that leads from one scene to the next, more often it is a visual link. Sometimes dialogue is 'folded over' into the next scene, that is to say, a line or two of dialogue continues over the opening visual of the next scene, but this is done in the editing and not something the writer need worry about.

At one time *the teaser* was quite popular and goes in and out of fashion quite regularly. This is simply a very strong hook used only at the opening, often prior to the main credits. The famous thriller series *The Avengers* used it. Here it was invariably a dead body found in some unusual circumstance — like hanging frozen from a meat hook or in a fountain in Trafalgar Square with a harpoon in its back.

Sing-song rhythms

It is very easy for dialogue to fall into a sing-song pattern, particularly in a question-and-answer sequence. Often you will not notice you are doing it until you go to the first reading, then it stands out a mile. You then find you have written half a dozen lines of roughly the same length and almost the same iambic structure. It arises from the same fault that I mentioned earlier, failure to visualize and retain characters with a separate identity.

Dialogue versus monologue

Directors naturally prefer dialogue to monologue since it gives them clear camera cutting points. Monologue makes them shudder since it implies static action. This can be a considerable restriction on writers who happen to be good at monologue construction. If you are a Harold Pinter they will accept it and put their minds to work to find new and interesting camera angles on the same face. But writing a good monologue is a rare skill since it involves a complex structure of changing thought patterns. It should not be confused with simple exposition. A character telling someone else what they had for breakfast in great detail, or explaining a complicated plot to the audience is not a legitimate use of monologue. If you use it at all, use it sparingly, and only for a climax speech. For all that, I am sorry that good monologue is not used more often in television, it is a great challenge.

Use of cliche

Naturally we all try to avoid it since it has such a bad name, but there is a great deal of humbug talked about its use. A cliche is really only a truism that has been used too often. In the limited vocabulary available to the television writer where Realism is the prevailing popular style, a certain amount of cliche is unavoidable. And it is not always the writer who indulges in it. There are director's cliches as well, and some directors have a quiver full. They are mostly in the order of shots — close up to reverse close up, to two shot to mid shot and back again, repeated ad nauseam is one kind of director's cliche. Many a good script has been ruined by director's cliches, many an indifferent one rescued from cliche by imaginative camera work.

A favourite visual cliche in television is the interminable exit line. A character starts to leave the set, then pauses and turns for his (or her) parting shot, then, since this has evoked a parting response —

another parting shot and so it can go on all night if you're not careful. Viz:

'Get out of here!'
'I'm going, don't worry.'
    (And makes for the door. Turns.)
'. . . but before I do, I just want to tell you something.'
    (Takes a step back into the room again.)
'I don't want to hear it.'
'Maybe not . . .'
    (Goes to exit again. Turns.)
'. . . but you're going to.'
    (Takes another step back into the room.)
'Joanna slept with *me* last night.'
'You're a liar!'
'OK. Then ask her.'
    (Goes to exit a third time. Pauses.)
'. . . and there's one other thing you should know.'
    and so on.

What the writer is now doing is writing a new scene and tacking it on to the first because he doesn't know where to stop. The effect is to confine one character in a static position while the other pops in and out like a cuckoo from a clock. He has forced the director into a cliche of movement.

In television there are a wide range of cliches available. Just try to keep the numbers down to manageable proportions.

One final plea on dialogue. Some actor has to speak those lines; before passing them over to him, make sure they are actually *speakable* by going over them in your head. In other words, mentally rehearse them yourself. Some lines may look terrific on paper, but they don't translate into fluent speech rhythms. If an actor trips over a clumsy line it can upset his timing. If he finds several dotted around the script it can throw him completely and he loses his performance. When that happens, your play is up the spout.

Chapter Six

Scenes — the Unit of Construction

A play is broken down into a number of scenes.

A play is *built up* from a number of scenes.

The two statements may seem to be saying the same thing, but they aren't. The first is the analytical approach, the second the creative approach. New writers often ask, 'How many scenes should the play (or series episode) contain?'

That question cannot be answered because it has been framed from the first assumption — that you start with a finite object of stated length, then break it down into its component parts. One might equally ask why there are separate scenes at all, why don't we just follow our principal characters wherever they go? To some extent, that is what happens when you write for films, as distinct from video. A number of small scenes are blocked together in continuous time — this is known as a *sequence*. When you write exterior action which will be made on film, then integrated back into the studio (video) production, you also write in sequences. A sequence might be described as a continuing event with a unity of time, but not of place. When laying down this sequence in the script, you will still do so in the form of scenes (indicating place, characters and movement with dialogue), and when they appear on screen they will seem to have been shot in one continuous action, but in fact they were probably separate camera 'set-ups' and may not even have been shot on the same day.

A typical sequence on film (or *Telecine,* as the BBC still quaintly calls it) may run as follows:

> Jack leaves his house, walks down the steps to the street, gets into his car and drives to Jill's house. He collects her and they drive to the Park. They then leave the car, walk to the pond, sit down on the seat and feed the ducks while expressing affection for each other or discussing the political situation in Afghanistan.

That is a very simple sequence involving only two people and will

33

look like one continuous piece of action on screen. But before that simple sequence can be shot, a number of production requirements have to be met.

Initially, a production manager will have to cost it. A location manager will have to find the areas you have indicated and make sure you can film there at all. Since an actor can't leave a house without having entered it first, the location manager will have to make sure he has found a house which is either empty, or the owner has given permission for it to be used. A designer has to make sure that the exteriors of both houses used will match the interiors (if used) that are being constructed in studio. If it is set in a busy metropolis where traffic never stops, arrangements will have to be made to ensure the streets are free to set up the camera and lighting equipment. When we reach the Park sequence, an area will have to be kept clear of passers-by and the crowds of small children who always gather the moment a camera crew arrives. The Sound Engineer will want to know whether there are likely to be obtrusive sources of unwanted sound — like low flying aircraft at frequent intervals or trains going by. Conversely, the script may have called for these things for dramatic reasons and although they can be laid on to the sound track afterwards, it may require a visual shot as well.

There are a number of other factors that have to be taken care of, like wardrobe and make-up, props, costumes, a 'dead' registration number for the car and bread for the ducks, but they need not bother the writer for the moment. The purpose of this catalogue of items and functions is to indicate the scope of preparation and detail needed to realize this simple sequence. Life will be made a great deal easier for all concerned if the events in the narrative are organized into scenes. Here is that same sequence as it would be laid down in script form.

| 1. | EXT. JACK'S HOUSE. FILM. DAY. | 1. |

JACK'S house is one of a terrace of shabby Victorian houses in a poor area of Wolverhampton. It is early morning. There are four full bottles of milk on the step and the newspaper is still stuck in the letterbox. The front door opens and JACK appears. JACK is about forty years old. A short, rotund Indian, with a warm, pleasant face and thinning hair. He is dressed in a light blue gaberdine summer suit and carries a raincoat over his arm. He ignores the newspaper, hurries down the step to the street where his car, a five-year-old saloon, is parked.

JACK opens the boot of the car, takes out a rag, polishes the windscreen and driving mirror, wipes off some flecks of dust from the body of the car, then, satisfied, gets into the driver's seat. He uses his rag to buff the passenger seat beside him carefully. Checks his appearance in the internal mirror and makes sure the ashtray is empty. Now satisfied, he buckles his seat belt and drives away.

3.   EXT. AVENUE. SUBURBS. FILM. DAY.   3.

A quiet, tree-lined avenue. The houses here are quite expensive, set back from the road and half hidden behind well manicured hedges. JACK'S car draws up beside the kerb. He gets out, adjusts his tie, glances at his finger nails to make sure they are clean, then walks on down the road.

4.   EXT. JILL'S HOUSE. FILM. DAY.   4.

The house, like the others in the Avenue, is set well back from the road with a gravel sweep approaching the front. A new Volvo estate car is parked in front of the garage.
JACK enters the drive, walks rather cautiously towards the front door, then hesitates. At that moment, the door opens and JILL hurries out. She is in her early twenties, tall, blonde haired and attractive. She is dressed casually in jeans and a sweater. She smiles, takes JACK'S arm. They hurry back to the road. When they are out of sight of the house, she kisses him on the cheek.

5.   EXT. PARK. FILM. DAY.   5.

The Park is quiet — just a few strollers with dogs. The trees are in full foliage. JACK'S car draws up. He gets out and hurries round to open the passenger's seat. But JILL is already out of the car. She takes his hand and they start to walk together across the grass.

6.   EXT. PARK. NEAR DUCKPOND. FILM. DAY.   6.

An empty wooden seat faces the pond. Beside it is an overflowing litter bin. CAM on some Muscovy ducks as they gather and jostle at the water's edge to be fed. WIDEN to show JACK and JILL seated on the park bench. JILL has taken some bread from her handbag, is breaking it up in her hand and throwing it to the ducks. JACK is seated rather self-consciously with his hands on his lap.

We now see that this one simple sequence has expanded into six scenes. So far not a word has been spoken, but you will notice that the characters have been filled out by small details of their appearance and behaviour — some by commission, some by omission. The viewers may read certain clues into these which will help them understand the characters and form an impression of this relationship.

For example, there were four full milk bottles on the doorstep, indicating that Jack does not live alone (or if he does he is a great milk drinker). His light suit indicated warm weather, possibly spring since he has taken a raincoat in case of showers. He did not take the newspaper out of the door. It was probably not his, indicating that he may only occupy a part of the house. He is concerned about both his own appearance and creating an impression of cleanliness by wiping down his car, and concern for his passenger by cleaning the seat. When he arrives at the street where she lives he parks his car some distance from her house. The difference in life-styles is apparent from the contrasting locations. The Volvo Estate parked outside the garage indicates a reasonably well-off, middle-class family. The fact that it is parked *outside* the garage may, for those who can read the signs, indicate that the garage is already full. A two, or possibly three car family and father definitely does not take priority when it comes to using the garage. His caution in approaching the house is now well understood. He is afraid he doesn't fit into this milieu. She also indicates a degree of embarrassment. She has clearly been waiting for his arrival and is anxious to get him out of sight of the house before showing any signs of affection. Finally, she knew where she was going since she brought bread for the ducks. This may indicate it is a familiar spot and not the first time they have met.

One can now see how the scenes that make up this sequence are used to feed a range of messages to the audience and give them time to absorb these messages. Meanwhile, back in the studio, another strand of this story is unfolding.

Use of studio

In the short film sequence I have just outlined, we had unlimited opportunities to take the narrative wherever we wished (always allowing for the budget limitations). There are only a limited number of sets that a studio will hold, usually five or six. The first thing the writer has to determine is how he can accommodate the story in the sets available. It is here that the production limitations condition the structure of the play itself. If there are two principals (as with the film sequence), each will presumably have a home. Even if we confine those homes to simple living rooms, that is two sets gone. If we want a bedroom, we have already used up half the studio space. The characters will need somewhere to meet outside the home. We may then have to create an office or place of work. They may need to relax or socialize with others so we create a pub, or social club. Now there is only space for one set left. Already the writer finds that the play is being shaped for him by the architecture. This is what I meant at the opening of this book when I referred to the limitations on imagery by the production process itself. The architecture is also beginning to shape and determine the scenes. It is hardly worth the huge expense of building and decorating a set if it is to be used once only. Twice round the studio floor and we already have twelve scenes mapped out, plus the six we have used up in the film sequence, plus perhaps another six for a similar sequence later in the development and we are into a couple of dozen whether we like it or not. Now the time factor is starting to operate. With an average of two minutes per scene, we have now filled a fifty minute slot (with a bit of space at each end for opening and closing title sequences). Already the initial question, 'How many scenes do I write?' is becoming largely academic. It is being decided for you. What you now have to avoid is making each of those scenes the same length or you will impose a deadly rhythm on the play that even the most skilled director cannot avoid. Of course there are no hard and fast rules. A fast action-packed thriller may rattle its way through fifty or sixty scenes; a one-off play where character development is the key factor may take no more than twenty.

A half-hour situation comedy may be told in ten scenes or less. While there are no fixed rules on scene construction, here are a few general guidelines which the new writer may find useful.

(1) Don't begin a scene until you have the shape of it clearly in your mind. Where possible, rehearse it in your head before committing it to paper. Know the point you are aiming at in each scene, don't just drift around hoping it will appear of its own accord.

(2) Don't try to convey too much *verbal* information in your early scenes. No-one's listening with any degree of concentration. Use these opening scenes to convey atmosphere, suspense, intrigue or impact. You can explain later.

(3) A scene must never mark time, but must always contain forward movement. This may not necessarily mean *physical* movement. There is movement in the unfolding of character; movement in discovery.

37

(4) Clearly visualize *all* the characters in a scene, don't just concentrate on the ones doing the talking. Much of the impact in drama is created by the reactions of characters to each other. Allow space for these reactions to take place.

(5) Try to avoid 'question and answer' dialogue. A scene is not a quiz. Even in straightforward interrogation scenes, people don't always answer the questions put to them. They are pursuing their own thoughts. The *way* in which a character responds, or fails to respond to a question can often be more revealing than the response itself.

(6) When a scene starts to bore *you* in the writing, it's a fair assumption that it is boring the viewer. When a scene starts to get 'sticky' and bogs down, throw it away and start again. Check back on the scenes leading up to it, that is where the fault may lie. Alternatively, you may have allowed a single line to lead the scene into a cul-de-sac. This is the error I mentioned earlier — letting the dialogue lead you by the nose.

Chapter Seven

Multi-strand Construction — Plots and Sub-plots

Although, in the space of fifty-odd minutes (which is the normal length for drama, thirty minutes for comedy), you only have time to tell one person's story — or two at the outside — the way in which you do so is rather like a tapestry weave. There are a number of threads to be woven together to create the complete picture. There are notable exceptions to this rule, particularly where the story is being told completely on film, but for the normal studio production with video-cameras and possibly a couple of film inserts, the multi-strand construction is the prevailing pattern.

But unlike the weaver, who may start with a number of threads of a set length laid out in front of him, the writer may do the reverse. He may start with a single thread — the spine of the story — then sub-divide it into its various component strands as he begins the weave.

To show this process in operation, it might be useful to go back to the exercise I mentioned on page 14, the premise given to the students at Arvon. In this case they began with a simple departure scene, the adolescent leaving home. We followed this up by asking them to concentrate now on two aspects of the event — the effect on the person leaving and the reactions on those left behind. It is a bit like the partition of an amoeba. Both cells now have an independent existence and we must follow their progress. On the one hand the person departing would find new people in a new setting. On the other, the parents left behind will react in a new way in the old setting. This may encompass relief, regret or mutual accusation. However they respond, their own lives will have been affected in some way which in turn will lead to certain developments. We now have a two-stranded story which we may follow through in alternate scenes. At some future point we may wish to bring those separate strands together again, but in pursuing them, we may introduce a third or a fourth strand. In several cases, the writer had introduced a boy-friend or girl-friend to whom the principal character had fled, or eloped with. In one case, the shock of the child leaving had brought about a crisis between the parents resulting in them splitting up to lead separate existences. In most cases one of the parents (usually the mother) attempted to pursue the child and win him or her back to the family fold, sometimes through an intermediary. But however the separate strands of the story developed, the writers were now obliged to pursue simultaneous lines of development, each having their own ambience (the set) and their own forward dynamic. Using the break-up of family unit as the starting point for multi-strand construction is one example, but there are infinite variations. It may be an individual leaving a large company to set up his own in rivalry, a man breaking out of custody to be hunted by his custodians or simply a chance meeting of strangers whose individual lives we then examine. Equally, we may start with two quite separate individuals and bring them together. In the example I used for creating scenes out of a sequence — the assignation between Jack and Jill — each will have their separate lifestyles and the characters contained in both may form the contrasting elements of the plot. Following the meeting in the Park it would have been natural to go to Jill's parents, or Jack's wife and family to pursue the narrative through their reaction. Alternatively, Jack may have been living alone and share his reactions with a confidant. The creation of a multi-strand plot looks simple enough, but it can get out of hand. Unless the number of characters either directly or marginally involved is kept under close discipline they can breed like rabbits, then each will need his or her place of abode and the half a dozen studio sets are used up in the first ten minutes of screen time.

In some cases, two people who appeared at first sight to be merely contributing marginally to the main plot may prove so interesting that we want to concentrate on their development — we cannot simply leave them in the air. This leads to a plot within a plot; following the same rules of construction — statement, counter-statement, conflict and resolution. This then becomes the sub-plot, and unless it is kept under control there is always a danger of it becoming the main plot. Often, when constructing a story, the characters in the sub-plot start to interest the writer more than the characters he started off with. He must then decide whether to relegate the first set of characters to a contributory role or scrap the whole thing and start again. Even when he thinks he has the balance just right, the play starts to take a different shape in production. If the director has cast two weak leads and a couple of outstanding character actors in the supporting roles, the entire emphasis of the play may change. This happens from time to time in series or serials. Certain characters, originally playing relatively minor roles, become so popular that they gradually take over the series. The producer will then insist that you write them up accordingly and the series can totally change direction; but I shall be dealing with the special problems of series writing in *Part II* of this book.

Creating a multi-strand plot, you will find, is not the difficult part. The real problem is keeping all the various elements in balance so that they contribute to, and strengthen the main line of story development. The function of the support roles, even when they take on the prominence of a separate sub-plot, is to illuminate the various facets of your main characters, and help them to tell the story. But keep them on a tight rein. Remember that once you have created additional characters they assume lives of their own, and given half a chance can elbow your principals off the stage.

Single strand development

Multi-strand plotting is by far the commonest construction technique, but not the only one. Just as on any publisher's list you may find both the intricately-woven novel and the biography or first person narrative, biographical drama also appears in the electronic publishers' schedules. This will tend to follow a single strand — the central character through a continuing series of events or cameo scenes. Although these are all called 'plays', they can differ widely in construction. Some might best be described as 'tele-journalism'.

While this book was being written, two programmes appeared in the box within a week of each other which neatly illustrate the difference between the journalist's style and the playwright's style. Both were dramatized biographies, and both, by coincidence, dealt with the same subject — the effect of solitary confinement on prisoners.

The first was a re-enactment of part of the life of Jimmy Boyle, the Glasgow gangster. For most of its length, the programme dealt with Boyle in various prison cells being beaten up by sadistic prison warders. But he was the hardest of hard cases and the only effect of this treatment was to stimulate counter-violence. Finally, in desperation, his gaolers gave up and he was transferred to Bairlinnie Prison where an enlightened governor practised the opposite approach — giving prisoners the maximum opportunity to socialize and lead reasonably normal lives. This method worked, and we are told by a superimposed caption at the end that Boyle's whole attitude was changed as a consequence. It was a vivid piece of documentary realism, superbly shot and lit. But in construction it contained little else but one scene of violence after another. There was no character change as a result — indeed, that was the point being made — but as a consequence, no sense of progression. It had ignored the traditional rules of dramatic structure, that the character shall undergo a change as a result of the events taking place. All conflict was external, the repetition of a sequence of scenes in which the prisoner was being beaten up. The play, in fact stood still. When the final caption appeared on screen to indicate that from this point on, Boyle's life had changed, millions of viewers must have felt that in some way they had been cheated; that this was almost the point where the story should begin, not end. Although they may have learnt something of the degree of violence that can take place in prisons, they knew little more about Boyle himself other than that he was a glutton for punishment.

This programme, incidentally, was produced for Scottish Television by Jeremy Isaacs, now Supremo of the 4th Channel, which may or may not give some indication of the kind of dramatic material this channel may favour.

The second programme, *The Jail Diary of Albie Sachs,* was written for the BBC by one of our most outstanding playwrights, David Edgar. In both cases, that of Boyle and Sachs, their captors tried to break the prisoner by prolonged solitude, but there the similarity ends. Whereas Boyle reacted violently to his conditions, so generating further violence, the South African lawyer's philosophy was non-violence. The central conflict was not, as with Boyle, two sides of the same coin, but a confrontation between two fundamentally-opposed philosophies. Sachs fought back with stubborn patience and an infinitely subtle capacity to ride every blow. The play became, therefore, a battle of ideas. At the same time, because of the diary form within which the play was constructed, we were able to follow Sachs's inner conflict, and his final resolution, to leave South Africa for ever, had been skilfully prepared by the playwright's artifice.

Two dramatized biographies, both in similar settings, prison, but *fundamentally* different in their approach. The first relying entirely on blunt physical impact, the second on a subtle interplay of characters. Both used a single strand approach, but the tune they played was very different.

Timing . . .
  How do I know how long it is?

Timing is crucial in television since everything has to fit tightly into scheduling slots. But how does the writer know when he is scripting it?

The seasoned professional does it by instinct, but since different directors will direct at different tempos, there can still be three or four minutes over-run or under-run on the same 50 minute script, depending on who is controlling the cameras.

The best guide for the beginner is to play it over in his head, literally acting all the parts, but that doesn't help with the stage or camera directions. Here you will have to play the part of the camera, seeing the picture as the camera, and therefore the audience, will see it, deciding in your own mind when the images presented have been given sufficient time to be absorbed. All this will come with practice, but as a rough and ready guide; a page of script as laid out in my example, typed on A4, is roughly a minute in playing time. So 50 minutes will come out at around 50 pages using a pica or elite typeface. If you have one of these fancy IBM's with justified lettering, it will come out rather longer than that.

If you want a final check, you may care to act the whole thing out on a tape recorder, describing the opening and closing camera descriptions verbally as the images pass across your mind's eye.

But don't worry too much if you are a bit overlength. Most scripts will tighten in the editing. It's better to be over length than under.

Camera Directions — How much do I need to know?

Most producers and directors will say very little. They want to tell the story their own way and don't welcome the writer trying to control them through the script. But like most things in television, it isn't quite as straightforward as that. You will notice in the scene breakdown for the Jack and Jill story, I indicated that I wanted the camera on the Muscovy ducks rather than on the two characters in Scene 6. I did this instinctively because I felt the sequence had gone on too long and I wanted to break it. The director would probably have done something similar in any case — possibly earlier in the sequence. If I had known who my director was going to be I probably wouldn't have bothered since I would be aware of his shooting style. But most writers never meet the director until the script is typed up ready for production — sometimes not until the actors' readthrough.

Despite directors' jealous protection of their own craft, it is sometimes necessary for the writer to indicate how he wants certain scenes played. To do this he must know at least some of the director's basic grammar. He must know, for example, where he wants the emphasis in a scene. It may be on an actor's face, it may equally be on a nervous reaction of the hands betraying what the face does not reveal. Some directors have a tiresome habit of pointing the camera in the direction of whichever character happens to be speaking at the time when you, for sound dramatic reasons, want that particular line to be off camera and the viewer to stay concentrated on the other character's silent reaction. If you feel strongly that this is how you want the scene played, *put it in the script*. There is no need to be technically precise as to how the effect is achieved. You may feel a strong need for a *close up,* the director may feel he can get a better effect by a half profile shot or even tracking in slowly. That is his business. But unless you indicate where you want the camera to favour, he may never know your intention. You may feel the need for one character to dominate a scene totally even though he may have very little dialogue. If so, put it clearly in the stage directions that this is how you want the scene played. If you are lucky, you will be given a director who can read subtleties in a script that you scarcely knew were there, and give an entirely new meaning to a scene by the skill with which he deploys his cameras. But you can just as easily be unlucky. I mentioned in the section on creating characters how your work can be influenced by the preceding set of characters who stay on after they should have been evicted from your mind. Directors can suffer from the same failing. Certain combinations of shots are retained in his memory from a previous production and even without being conscious of it, a director can impose them on a script for which they are entirely unsuitable.

It is up to you, the writer, to indicate the way in which you originally envisaged the play to the director. If you fail to do so, you have only yourself to blame if he interprets it quite differently.

Above all, you must see with the eye of a camera, remembering that it has no peripheral vision. It can only see what it is looking at directly. Despite the variety of angles that can be achieved in studio by a four or five camera set-up, or by several takes from different angles by the film camera on location, the camera is still a relatively blunt instrument compared with the subtle complexity of the human eye. So make sure it knows where you want it to be looking. See it first in your mind's eye, then convey that picture as accurately as you can to paper. Don't worry if you don't know the technical terms for achieving the effect you want, just put it in your own language.

Occasionally a director will carry out the author's intentions so faithfully that he will even try to stage typing errors. I was once called in half way through a rehearsal and asked if I would mind if a character could use a broom instead of a vacuum cleaner as the implement was causing difficulties with the sound balance. I looked at him blankly and said that I had not asked for a vacuum cleaner. He pointed to the script where it said 'Mary is hoovering by the door.' Obedient to instructions, the production manager had ordered a hoover from the props department and they had been using it for three hours before conceding that there was no

way of doing it without drowning the dialogue. I produced my
original script. 'The line,' I said, 'is *hovering* by the door.'

But for those who wish to include a few technical terms in the script,
the following is a glossary of the more common terms:

C.U.	Close-up. Where the face fills the screen.
B.C.U.	Big Close-up. Showing only a part of the face.
M.S.	Medium shot (or Mid-shot). Half the figure — above the waist.
M.L.S.	Medium Long Shot. Showing the complete figure, or group of figures at close range.
L.S.	Long Shot. Figures at a distance (or objects at a distance).
2S (or Two-shot)	Two figures in the frame.
Pan	Where the camera moves laterally from one character to the other, from a character to to an object or vice-versa.
Whip-pan	The same movement at higher speed.
Tracking shot	The camera moving with the character(s), or in towards them.
Pull back	The camera moving back from the characters (or object)
Tighten	Going in towards them. Distinct from the tracking shot in that it is usually a change in focal length rather than the camera moving physically.
High angle/ low angle	Exactly what they imply. Used more on film than in studio since the height is not always available on the set.
Ext. Exterior. Int. Interior Int/Ext	is often used when the scene encompasses shots both inside and out — as, for example, getting into or out of a vehicle.
Cut	Directors don't like you telling them where to cut, they consider it their business. But writers often use *Cut to:* when they wish to draw particular attention to a character or object. There is no need to put it at the end of every scene as this is obvious, unless you particularly want to indicate a sharp cut rather than a *Mix*.
Mix	is a cross fade from one scene to another where the images merge rather than change

	abruptly. Less used these days than in the past.
Resume	Returning to the point at which you left a scene after cutting to another scene. It assumes no change in the physical disposition of the characters in the scene and often very little change in time.
DAY/NIGHT	Either one or the other is always included in the scene heading. This is not just a convention, night shooting involves all kinds of special logistic and lighting problems, so use it sparingly. If you wish for a special dawn or dusk effect, indicate DAY (FOR DAWN) or DAY (FOR DUSK). But remember that the sun doesn't stand still waiting for long scenes to be played. It is at most an effect for the opening of a scene, or a short closing sequence. Used for film only.
SFX	Sound effect(s). Use only when you want a particular sound effect that affects the dramatic content. Normal background sound can be safely left to the Sound Engineer.
OS. (or OOV)	Out of shot (or Out of Vision). Where there is dialogue from a character not in vision. Not to be confused with:
V.O.	Voice over, which, strictly speaking, means spoken narrative laid on to the scene afterwards in the Sound editing.
Filter	Where the voice is distorted by technical apparatus, as through a telephone receiver or loudspeaker. Occasionally referred to as *Distort* when other means of distorting the voice are used.
P.O.V.	Point of view. Literally where you wish the camera to see what your character is seeing. The instruction: CUT *to his/her* POV is quite commonly used, but the writer usually forgets to put the REVERSE shot back to the character. The better directors dislike this instruction as they may have more interesting ways of following the character's eyeline, but it is a convenient piece of shorthand.

CAPTIONS, CREDITS	The title of the play or series episode plus the names of the actors, writer, director, etc.
SUPER CAPTIONS	Not giant versions of the above. The word super is merely an abbreviation for superimpose.
FADE TO BLACK	The moment of bliss. The script is finished. But many of your problems are just beginning. I shall be dealing with a few of these in Part Two.

Part Two

Chapter Eight

Medium and Message . . .

>What do I want to say?
>And will they let me?

> 'If you've got a message, take it to Western Union.'
> Legendary advice to Hollywood writers in the Thirties

The idea that there is 'pure entertainment' on the one hand and socially committed or 'message' drama on the other does not really stand up to serious scrutiny. The huge output of escapist films from the Hollywood dream factories in the thirties and on through to the mid-fifties may have appeared to be pure entertainment on the surface, but taken as a whole it conveyed a wide range of social and political messages.

One of the most prevalent themes — the 'rags to riches' story — conveyed the social message that virtue was its own reward and hard work and individual enterprise automatically led to happiness. When Orson Welles, in *Citizen Kane,* shattered this idyll by conveying the counter message, that the acquisition of wealth led to loneliness and isolation, it came as such a cultural shock that he was considered a subversive. By designating him as such, the Hollywood moguls were tacitly admitting that they themselves were pursuing an ideology — the American (or specifically Californian) way of life

— to which the message implicit in *Citizen Kane* appeared as heresy. The pretence of 'pure entertainment' values was now exposed. You cannot proclaim a heresy unless you subscribe to an ideology or creed in the first place. The arraignment of the famous 'Hollywood Ten' during the McCarthy era, and the savagery with which they were attacked, proved beyond any measure of doubt that entertainment was not removed from the political arena, but considered an integral part of it. The advocates of pure entertainment had been hoisted on their own petard.

The post-war changes that have taken place in the structure of society have, in greater or lesser degree, been reflected in entertainment. Because we can now see the products of four or five decades alongside one another in a single evening on the television screen, it is relatively easy to identify the messages they contain and see them for what they are — the propaganda of the epoch. The most noticeable changes in the United States have been the changes in attitudes towards the role of women, and towards ethnic minorities, American Negroes in particular. The *Küche-Kinder-Kirche* role of women in the early movies is now rightly identified by the Feminist movement as blatant male chauvinist propaganda. The Paul Robeson role in *Sanders of the River* as Uncle Tom racism. It must therefore follow that what appears on the surface to be the most harmless 'non-message' fiction of one era will appear as ideological propaganda to the next. In Britain, where the divisions in social classes are measured by a complex pattern of vocal intonation and mannerisms, the most obvious change has been in the selection of characters as source material. Whereas they were once predominantly upper-middle-class with clipped voices and long vowel sounds, they are now drawn from all social classes and the centre of gravity has moved North of Watford. Women are no longer simple housewives and Blacks all bus conductors. It would be simple to interpret these changes in screen images simply as a natural reflection of changes in society, but they are more contrived than that. The significant increase in the number of American Blacks and representatives of other ethnic minorities in everything from San Francisco cop shows to situation comedies was not a natural growth. It was a positive instruction from the Heads of the Networks, reacting to political pressure. The inclusion of women in leading roles where they motivate the principal action (even to the point where they assume superhuman physical powers, as in *Wonderwoman*) was a policy decision responding to pressure from the Women's Rights Movement. The U.S. series *Bonanza* was compounded from a policy decision to cast each of the principal actors as representative of a distinct ethnic type, from swarthy Latin to blonde Nordic, even though all the sons were supposed to have come from the same father. The contrasting physical types of Starsky and Hutch was another policy casting decision. The same process is happening in British television today, both previously under represented groups, women and characters from ethnic minorities are being given prominence in the drama output *as a matter of policy.*

Indeed, and why not? Surely it is the responsibility of the visual media to take the lead in helping the audience towards racial harmony and an end to patriarchal attitudes. Every enlightened liberal must applaud this role for the audio-visual media, but the significant phrase is 'taking the lead'. In short, television is consciously and as a matter of deliberate policy projecting social attitudes in order to advance public understanding. To that extent it is evasive to pretend, as some senior company executives *do* pretend, that they are simply concerned with pure entertainment values and reject written material containing 'messages'. What they are actually rejecting is messages they either do not agree with or have not been obliged, by the prevailing social climate, to accept.

Since many writers do feel they have something significant to say, and are not just content to entertain *in vacuo,* it might be useful to list some subjects and areas where companies (at the time of writing) either feel distinctly nervous of certain themes, or will only accept them subject to substantial cosmetic surgery.

In attempting to define these areas, it must be remembered that different commercial television stations have different policies, and that even within those companies, a change of Programme Controller can predicate a change of attitude — either for better or for worse. Much the same applies to the BBC. The Programme Controller of BBC2 may accept something that has been rejected by his opposite number on BBC1. What I am trying to do here is to give an indication of the kind of subjects where television as a whole is either extremely sensitive or plainly censorious, and I suppose we must start with the obvious since it is the one which invariably receives the greatest publicity.

Dat veniam corvis, vexat censura columbas.
(Censure acquits the raven, but pursues the dove — Juvenal)

Sex 'n Violence

Except in the case of rape, where extreme violence is used for sexual ends, it is hard to understand how these two aspects of human behaviour ever became linked in the first place. They are at the two extreme ends of the moral spectrum. Violence is a product of hatred and cruelty, sexual attraction, of love. Where people take their clothes off, either on or off screen, it is invariably to invite tenderness and caress, and how this can be considered offensive or disgusting remains a total mystery to me. The usual claim by the objectors to scenes of nudity, that they are protesting on behalf of children, and not in their own cause, has always seemed to me to be transparently dishonest. It is a Tom Tiddler's ground for humbug and repressed sexuality on the part of the protestors. It is also significant that the most voluble defenders of the morals of children either seem to have none of their own or are too old to remember how children react to the human body. Nevertheless, the anti-sex and nudity lobby is now a considerable pressure group and has the Television executives running scared. Puritanism is back in vogue, and since it invariably thrives in times of insecurity, fear and economic uncertainty, new writers should be warned that the pendulum is likely to swing even further in this direction over the next few years.

Pornography is a horse of a different colour, but the word itself needs careful definition. Strictly speaking it means writing about harlots, and if taken literally could apply to a wide range of literature from *'Tis a Pity She's a Whore* to *The Lady of the Camellias*. But in common parlance it is taken to mean brutalization of sexuality by display or description and the degradation of women. In this respect it is a form of violence and should properly be placed under that category. It should not be confused with erotica, which has a respectable pedigree.

As to physical violence, acts of cruelty and brutality of a non-pornographic nature, little need be said except that people usually turn to violence when they lack the capacity to be articulate, and it is fundamental to the writer's craft to make the inarticulate, articulate. In this light, resorting to violence in a script may be seen as a failure on the writer's part to exercise his skill with words. In practice, many of the violent scenes on television were either inserted, or at least elaborated, by directors looking for visual excitement. But it is usually the writer who is accorded the blame.

Bad language . . .

It could be said that there is no such thing as bad language, there are only bad people, and they can be bad in any language. But what most people are talking about when they use this term are words and phrases that have become taboo in the particular age in which we live. Generally the term is confined to common language descriptions for sexual activity, the reproductive organs or, occasionally, words that offend religious susceptibilities. As with nakedness and explicit love making, it is only fair to warn new writers that the television censors are now far more active than they were in the late Sixties and early Seventies, and scripts containing words over which there may be any doubt or argument

51

are now referred upstairs to higher authority as a matter of course. The fact that the same words and phrases as may appear in your script may be used in every other sentence by the censors themselves, should not lull you into a false sense of security. As Sydney Newman once said to me when I was protesting at the degree of censorship in the BBC on behalf of the Writers Guild, 'Aw shit, Eric, you know fucking well we can't use bad language!'

But the variety of permissible language depends a great deal on the time of night your work is scheduled for transmission. The following is a rough guide as things stand at the moment, though once again, they will vary with the company: 'Bloody' is out before 10 p.m., but all right from then till closing time. 'Shit', 'Sod' and 'Piss off!' are allowed from 11 o'clock on, but mainly in single one-shot plays. 'Bastard' is OK in Scotland after ten, but in England only after eleven. This is because the Scots are supposed to go to bed earlier than the English (though I'm not sure what happens in Berwick-on-Tweed).

All the rest are out unless you can prove they are germane to the artistic integrity of the work — which you can't, of course, since you aren't the one who's making the judgement, *they* are.

Actually, most of the arguments advanced for the protection of the nation's children from learning words they use every day in the school playground are somewhat specious. The main reason why programmes have been 'cleaned up' over recent years is in response to requests from the overseas salesmen. Most drama, particularly the series and serials, is now offered for sale to those parts of the world where there is an even greater degree of humbug — the United States, Canada, Australia and New Zealand. One 'Up your arse, Nigel' in the pilot programme could ruin the sale potential of the entire series.

Notwithstanding these words of caution, if you feel it necessary to put forms of expression in the mouths of your characters for which any euphemism would sound false or contrived, do so. And don't take the opinions of producers, directors or story editors as gospel. They often prefer to err on the side of caution. Insist that you get a ruling from the top.

But having nailed your colours firmly to the mast on the right and duty of the dramatist to use language appropriate to his characters, there is another side to the case which often gets lost in the heat of the argument. A surfeit of expletives can impoverish a drama, rendering the characters repetitive and boring. In Realist drama, writers too often use the adjectival expletive because they are too lazy to think up a colourful alternative. Don't fall into the trap of making all your characters so limited in their range of speech that they become typecast clones. Very ordinary people have far more poetry in their minds than they are willing to articulate. It is part of the dramatist's job to find means of expression for this imagery. I remember a heated argument I

52

once had with a producer about a character I had written into a popular serial, a milk roundsman who recited Yeats to keep his spirits up in wet weather. 'My milkman', the producer insisted, 'wouldn't even know who Yeats was.' 'He's not *your* milkman,' I said. 'He's *my* milkman. I created him and he'll speak as I choose.'

I finally won the argument at script level but lost it in production. When it came to the filming they smothered all his dialogue in a clatter of milk bottles.

Chapter Nine

Ideas — Acceptable and Unacceptable . . .

In the mid-Sixties I wrote a play for ATV called *The White Rhino*. It told the story of a white Inspector of Schools who had spent most of his life in Central Africa. After independence, he returns to the UK to try to find a job he considers suitable to his talents and experience. During the course of the play he is forced to realize that Britain has changed radically from his memory of it as a boy. He is approaching retirement age and no-one wants a man whose concepts of education are firmly set in the Colonial era. Finally he is reduced to working in the battery sheds of a chicken farmer in order to pay his drinks bill. In the final scene he is to shoot himself, ignominiously, behind the chicken shed. But the night before he dies he makes a speech to the indifferent and puzzled regulars in the local pub, expressing his philosophy of life. In this final, defiant statement, he condemns egalitarian society, pointing out that all the cultural riches we now enjoy were created by multiple tier societies — from the Athenian slave state (spuriously called a democracy), through the Pharaonic, Roman and finally British Empire. Our present society, he claims, with its insistence on equal rights for all citizens, will leave nothing for posterity but waste and ignorance.

Since this was not a popular philosophy, particularly in the late Sixties, I had a fight on my hands to keep this speech in, the company representatives pointing out that this was an historical justification for *apartheid*. The speech, they claimed, being followed by the man's suicide would create sympathy for the character and therefore sympathy for his viewpoint. Could I not tone it down a little, indicating that the character now realized he was wrong? I refused, arguing that the character must remain true to his own beliefs and the whole point of the tragedy lay in the fact that he could *not* adapt. I won, or I thought I had won. But clearly this had troubled the production team all the way through the rehearsal period and the director finally came up with the answer. I was, he decided, being immensely subtle. What I meant to imply was that the man was talking gibberish, so he directed his leading actor to play it as an incoherent drunk shouting inanities to a noisy crowd who drowned most of the content of the speech with rhubarb. And that is how it appeared on the box, with not a line changed but the dramatic impact of the key speech completely distorted.

In the censorship of ideas, there are more ways than one of skinning a cat.

But themes and ideas do not have to stray into the field of sex, unacceptable language or the polemics of politics to be considered dangerous or unacceptable. There are certain 'protected areas' that the writer can only enter with extreme caution. The medical profession is just such hallowed ground. Whereas it is now grudgingly accepted that occasionally a doctor may be portrayed as making a wrong diagnosis, the idea that he could equally be lazy, incompetent, drunk, an indifferent dispenser of pills, cruel to his wife or dog (most particularly his dog) would have the blue pencils out in no time at all. Religion has always enjoyed special status, though often with curious logic. A play depicting a parish priest interfering with choirboys may be acceptable, since it is part of popular newspaper mythology that this is what parish priests get up to from time to time, but a serious play, however finely written, which makes out a strong case for the ethics of atheism or agnosticism would stand a very thin chance. The police and legal profession no longer enjoy the special protected status that they had at one time, but just try submitting a play about a corrupt magistrate or an incompetent Judge!

Old age and natural death is yet another subject that you treat at your peril. Although it is an acceptable convention that a score of fictional characters a week can be gunned down, blown up, poisoned, pushed off cliffs or otherwise casually slain, a dramatic study of how to face up to the foreknowledge of death, the afterlife (or absence of it) would be considered a subject likely to cause alarm and despondency.

Ironically, period drama is full of tragedy, since it has always been one of the two foundation stones of the art itself. Most of the classic novels contain the tragic element, and when they are adapted for the small screen, no-one would dream of editing it out. But when we come to original contemporary drama, tragedy is somehow considered downbeat rather than purgative or elevating. Which is not to say you should not attempt it — simply be warned that a realistic portrayal of death on screen in a modern setting is likely to make Drama Departments distinctly nervous.

But so far I have been dealing with straight drama; when we come to comedy, many of these strictures disappear.

55

In the example I gave of the exercise set for the students at Arvon, I mentioned that some of the writers automatically turned to comedy when they found the subject uncomfortable or distressing. This was hardly surprising since television does exactly the same thing. Politics are a joke, sex is a joke, death is a joke and the bumbling old incompetent Judge is practically a stock character. All the 'protected professions', in fact, where in straight drama you would be walking on glass, you are quite free to send up in comedy.

But beneath the joke, writers often convey quite serious messages and are able to make quite trenchant comments on the structure of society. If Johnny Speight, creator of *Till Death Do Us Part,* had submitted a straight play with *Alf Garnet* as a central character, it would have been winging its way back to his agent in very short time.

In comedy, most subjects are available for treatment and acceptable provided they are funny and whatever social comments they contain are disguised by mirth.

The tradition of granting a special licence to comedy writers is an ancient one, dating back in Britain to mediaeval times. They are the modern equivalent of the King's fool, or court jester. Like *Poor Tom* in *King Lear,* they fulfil a vital function in reflecting the funny side of madness or distress. But there are set limits even for the licenced jester. Let them *cease* to be funny, or penetrate too deeply beneath the skin and they will feel the sharp edge of the axe as surely as any straight playwright.

Precensorship . . .

With all these restrictions, limitations, delicate areas and prohibitions, you might ask why we don't hear more of censorship on the box? From time to time the odd case gets publicity — like Peter Watkins' *The War Game,* Roy Minton's *Scum,* Dennis Potter's *Brimstone and Treacle* or Ian McEwan's *Solid Geometry,* but considering the huge output from the box, isn't this the exception rather than the rule?

The short answer is that these were the fish that slipped through the net. These plays actually *got made* so there was something to shout about. Most controversial subjects don't get past the producer's desk in script form, so if they are rejected, no-one can ever prove they would have made good plays in the first place. Somewhat unfairly, it is usually the BBC that finds itself at the centre of any storms over censorship, while the commercial companies generally keep out of trouble. But this should not be taken as proof that the Corporation has the heaviest hand, quite the contrary. It is simply that the BBC has traditionally given its producers and heads of departments a looser rein in the past. (It is tightening up a lot now, I regret to say.) In an organization that size, the watchdogs can't keep an eye on everything that is going on in the production departments. The smaller companies can, and do.

But that is only part of the reason for a diet of bland television; the deeper and more disturbing reason is that most writers *censor themselves.* Professional writers in particular, with mortgages to pay, families to support and taxmen to pay off know, because they study the market, that certain subjects, or ways of treating subjects, will not be acceptable in advance. Few writers can afford the luxury of spending five or six weeks working on a play they know, or their agents will warn them, won't get to air.

Pre-censorship becomes a habit. The writer finds he is automatically aborting ideas from his mind before they are even born. Or, if he is convinced he has a good one that won't make the box, he will save it for the stage, a film or a novel.

In this respect there is a great virtue in innocence. The new writer will not know the market so well, he probably hasn't even got an agent yet who can cool his ardour with pragmatic advice. And the *brave* new writer will treat everything I have said so far on the subject of censorship with a pinch of salt. He (or she) will do it *his* way and damn the consequences.

It should also be said, if not too cynically, that a few of the old hands know a trick worth two of that. In publicity terms, and quite often in financial returns, it can sometimes be a positive advantage to get your play banned. Many a good playwright has laboured anonymously for years at his craft until one day he gets that lucky break. His play is banned and becomes a *cause celebre.* Now, at least he is known. He is now a controversial playwright, and since there will probably be a film offer for the banned subject within the next twenty-four hours, he can confidently protest all the way to the bank.

But it takes a lot of ingenuity and a fair amount of luck to find the hole in the net in the first place. Unproduced plays aren't news.

This is the big one . . .
        but will they recognize it?

You watch the box, examine the drama output and decide that the current popular fare is not your scene at all. You have seen one costume drama, you have seen the lot. The endless diet of marital infidelities, cop shows, petty villains and mini-heroes appear trivial and inconsequential compared with the major issues of our time. You look at the news headlines and see confrontations of massive proportions; the world is on the brink of nuclear war; millions are starving while others have a surfeit of food; irreplaceable forms of life are being destroyed for ever by pollution; military or political dictatorships commit their citizens to inhuman torture and imprisonment — the world has gone mad and the individual seems powerless to prevent disaster. Even on the local, domestic scene there are issues that seem to be crying out for the dramatist to portray — millions are unemployed, our industries are being closed down through blind adherence to economic heresies, our education system is collapsing, we are being led by false prophets headlong back into the Dark Ages.

In any one of these themes there are, surely, all the elements for *big scale* drama, equal to the Titanic struggles between men and Gods that created the dynamic for the timeless drama of Sophocles or Euripides.

So why the Hell isn't someone writing it for the greatest auditorium of all time — the television screen?

It would be too easy to answer that there just doesn't happen to be a Sophocles or a Homer around right now, or that we are all so illiterate we have not their command of language. What you are really talking about is the immensity of the *idea.* Couldn't we at least *try* to tackle themes at this level, even if we do it badly?

It is true, of course, as I mentioned earlier in this book, that the documentary feature programmes have taken these as their own domain, leaving little but the crumbs for the dramatist. But that is to beg at least three questions: firstly, *why* have the dramatists ceded the feature men the high ground? Secondly, can the feature programme ever have the emotional impact of the drama and thirdly, are they really covering the ground at all, or merely nibbling at the edges of a limited range of permissible subjects?

There are as many answers as there are questions, but the general proposition — that television drama is not matching up to the challenge of our times, is certainly valid.

Now let's come down to earth.

Assuming the subject matter is acceptable, the first thing the writer must do with any grand scale idea is to focus it down on characters. It cannot be repeated too often that drama is about people, not philosophical concepts. You will have to select characters who are both capable of bearing the weight of the arguments you want to present and, by virtue of their occupations, motives or inescapable circumstances, *central* to the conflict. Any old people just won't do, certainly not randomly selected people wearing the playwright's hat.

They will need to be people whose lives are fundamentally affected by the issues involved, not just intellectually, but emotionally. Emotion is the carrier wave which will convey your story message to the audience, and imprint itself on *their* emotions. If the play is not an emotional experience for the audience it will have no impact, however important the issues involved, or however elegantly phrased.

Alternatively, you may decide to approach the theme from the other end — not those affected by the issue, but those affecting it, the manipulators rather than the manipulated. To take the first of the suggested issues, if you want to set your play in the shadow of an atomic holocaust, you may find it more profitable to focus on the people making the fatal decisions rather than those who will suffer from them. Bernard Shaw, of course, would contrive to have them both on the same stage, but not everyone is a G.B.S. Shakespeare used Kings, Princes, Consuls and Tyrants as the lynchpins of his works not, as some historians have suggested, because he relied on the aristocracy for patronage but because they were the people who made the vital decisions. In general, viewers prefer to see the decision-makers on stage, they like to feel that they are at the heart of events, but it is up to you to decide where that heart lies.

Having determined your principal characters, you must now decide where to put them. Although in any really great play, the setting will disappear, in lesser drama it can substantially affect your characters — either by adding to their strength or detracting from it. Many a powerful speech has been spoilt by pretty wallpaper in the background or knick-knacks on the mantelpiece. Tell the designer what you want and the effect you are trying to create. Most television designers are bored stiff with the same old domestic settings anyway and will welcome your suggestions. Lighting men also rise to a challenge, and in Britain we have the finest lighting technicians in the world.

So choose the sets in your mind's-eye carefully. They must be essential to the plot, but within those limits they can still add a great deal to the impact the characters have on the audience.

It should be mentioned at this point that a lot of new technology is being brought into use in television at the moment, particularly in the creation of new dimensions in settings. If you have watched *The Hitch Hiker's Guide to the Galaxy* on the box you will have seen what can now be done with video-electronic gadgetry. Don't bank on getting all that expensive and complex equipment for *your* play, but be aware that the visual architecture is now far more flexible today and this will affect the shape of plays in the future.

Having set up the people and the place, you must now consider the period of time within which the story is to be told. Audiences are now very sophisticated in their acceptance of time changes, but there is a general rule that the shorter the time span, the tighter and more effective the result. We have now observed two of the so-called *Aristotelian Unities* (in fact, Aristotle only ever mentioned two — unity of time and action, the third, unity of place, was invented by the French in the seventeenth century).

Now it's time for the action, and it is at this point the writer starts to realize that the world-shaking revelations he intended to convey just won't obey the rules. They are essentially static thoughts. Worse still, they are starting to disperse as the characters take over and start to lead lives of their own, reacting to each other's behaviour, wandering off into other avenues of thought — like rebellious schoolchildren at a dry lecture. It is no use the dramatist shouting at them to pay attention with a few erudite speeches. Instead of being absorbed in the magnitude of the theme, they are now flicking emotional ink blobs at each other.

The mistake he has made is to try to impose *his* views on the characters instead of developing ideas through them. They have got bored and switched off, and because by this time they now represent the audience, the viewer has switched off too.

So how did those old Greeks manage the trick? Firstly they were not dealing with new and innovative ideas. Greek tragedy was not drawn from contemporary themes, but from myths that everyone in the amphitheatre had been familiar with from childhood. They were *received* ideas, and much of the fabric of the play was a ritual exposition of them. The audience had therefore built up an expectation of the events in the narrative and were not being called upon to absorb a whole litany of new concepts.

This is beginning to sound like a dismal excuse for keeping things as they are, operating only within the viewers' preconceptions. Partly so, but not entirely. New and radical thinking can, and must, be introduced into television drama, but it is only effective when there is a groundswell of opinion already forming in the audience's consciousness. The writer with his antennae properly tuned will sense that movement and crystallize it. It is largely a matter of timing.

> There is a tide in the affairs of men, which, taken at the flood leads on to fortune . . .

Omitted, and they'll all be switching over to Sportsnight.

Chapter Ten

The Bread and Butter . . .

Most new writers break in with the 50-minute single play, but there are too few play slots to provide a reasonable income. The bulk of the work available on the box is in the form of Series and Serials.

Definitions

A *Series* is a sequence of episodes pursuing a central theme and/or principal characters, in which each episode tells a story complete in itself. Series are usually 50 minutes in length (for the BBC, approximately 52 minutes for the commercial stations) in drama, 30 minutes (26 minutes for commercial) for situation comedy.

A *Serial* is much the same but with a continuing story line. The Serial episode can be either 30 or 50 minutes (or the commercial variations thereof) and are usually prepared in segments of 13 episodes.

There is also the *Closed Serial,* that is usually an original work, with story and characters provided by the one writer and is really a long play broken up into episodes. On average they run for six episodes, but will vary as to subject. The six-part thriller serial comes in and out of fashion. Dramatizations of literary works will be of whatever length the original work will stand without becoming too drawn out.

There is also a hybrid form called the Series/Serial — no-one has yet thought of a less clumsy name for it. This is basically a Serial, but although the underlying narrative continues from week to week, each episode contains a plot which is complete in itself. The form was created mainly because of problems in selling Serials overseas — some countries may not take the full 13 episodes but prefer to lift some episodes out, not necessarily in order. The magic number 13, incidentally, was not chosen because it is unlucky, but as a scheduling convenience. The 52 weeks of the year are apportioned into four 13 week segments.

Constructing a Series or Serial

Some Series and Serials are created 'in house', that is to say, by producers or editors on either staff or renewable programme contracts. There is a certain attraction to the Corporation or Company in this arrangement since it means they may have some degree of copyright interest in the format and characters, and certainly have more artistic control. But since drama and comedy writers are not carried on staff (though there are quite a few people inside who *think* they are writers), the actual scripting will be done by freelances working at home and carrying all their own overhead costs. In Series, the freelance writer will provide his own story line for each episode and may create new characters as the Series changes shape during the course of development. In this event, the new characters are the copyright property of the particular writer who created them and the resulting copyright position can often be somewhat complicated. Broadly speaking, it is easiest to regard the position of being one of a shared copyright — which means that neither party can exploit the property outside the medium for which it was intended without the permission of the other.

But with the notable exception of *The Avengers* and *Dr Who*, few 'in house' Series have been spectacularly successful. Most of the well-loved Series have come from formats either submitted or commissioned from the freelance market, and long may it remain so. The danger of too many in-house series is that they become incestuous, a regurgitation of the same ideas in different dress or a conscious attempt to repeat the successes of yesteryear. (It is often said of BBC Television Centre that it was built in the shape of a circle so that the same ideas could travel around and around like an echo chamber.)

Some Series or Serial formats are put together by outside 'packaging' agencies, notably *The Brothers, The Expert, Colditz* and *Secret Army*. In these cases the writer and producer were put together by the agent, who then leased the copyright in the format to the BBC. But the commissioning of writers to work on them was under the control of the Corporation and several writers from other agencies were engaged for subsequent episodes and the packaging exclusivity was confined to the original format only.

The banking Serial *Telford's Change* was also put together from the outside, in this instance as a 'co-operative' between writer, director and leading actor, but throughout television as a whole, the market is still open to independent submissions from writers who are neither part of a package, or have a useful contact on staff. The first thing you will need is what is called *the format*.

Basically this is a general statement of the idea or theme. This should be reasonably brief, establishing the general ambience of the Series, the period in which it is set, the central locations from which it is based, the principal characters who will be used throughout the Series and, above all, the conflict implicit in the idea itself. Keep it in straightforward, simple prose, if you start breaking into dialogue to explain what you want, you will ramble on forever. You will have to use a certain amount of 'colouring' to grab the attention of the busy producer or editor, but don't overdo it with purple prose or what is effectively advertising copy. No-one is fooled by sentences like:

> 'This series vividly portrays the life and death struggle between vibrantly beautiful gossip columnist Marcia Kettledrum and her ex-husband, craggy, steely-eyed Sir Kemsley Murdoch, as they use every dirty trick known to Fleet Street to destroy each other's careers.'

It is certainly a fact that a well known Programme Controller once bought a drama series on the basis of a format containing the following breathless promise:

> 'Oh . . . we will make our enthusiasm infectious so that we will surf forward on a tidal wave of fun!'

But the tide went out after the statutory first 13 episodes and it was quietly buried. The Programme Controller has now been moved upstairs where he can keep his feet dry.

Don't waste too much time setting up the people in the general synopsis, because you will now move on to the more interesting section — describing the characters. You need only confine yourself to the Principals, but these should be described in depth and their relationships fully explored.

It is here that you will find the format for a Series tends to differ from that of a Serial. Most *Series* are centred around a very small number of principal characters — it may be only one. The story material will arise from how they motivate, react to or generally impel the action of each episode, usually by virtue of their chosen profession. (Policeman, doctor, private eye, prison governor, et alia.) The burden of the format will therefore be in the final section — the outline of each episode, the stories themselves. It is useful to describe the opening story outline (the pilot script) in scene breakdown. The next two episodes need not be in such detail but should be fairly fully described. To show that the idea has further potential, prepare at least another three outlines to follow, though these may be in abbreviated form.

A format for the *Serial* is a more complex document. Firstly you will have to create a wider range of characters, even if some may not appear until the second, third or even sixth episode, if they are going to be a vital part of the general weave of the narrative, they must be described in detail. Once again, the first episode outline must be given in full, the second and third in some detail, but after this you will have to project ahead to the full 13. You have set characters in motion, interwoven their destinies, and the producer will want to know the roles they will play throughout, in particular, whether you have really thought them through.

Creating a format for what you hope will be a long running Serial is much harder than it looks. Every character has to have the potential for continuing involvement and development. In one way or another they must be locked together so that they can continue to react one upon the other. They may be forced together by family involvement, their place of work or a mutually essential point of assembly, some kind of *Deus ex Machina* which obliges them to interact, or more usually, a combination of all these factors.

Half-a-dozen foolscap pages may be sufficient to present a format for a Series, but you will be lucky if you can get a full Serial format in less than 20. A situation comedy format may be a simpler document, since it is essentially about getting the right mix of characters in the right setting, but it is unlikely that a new writer will be able to sell on a format alone. It gives little indication as to whether he can actually write comedy dialogue. If you are trying to sell comedy, it is wise to write and submit a full script unless you are already well known. This should be accompanied by half-a-dozen brief story outlines to indicate that there is more in it than a single idea.

Growth and change . . .

It is quite rare for a Series or Serial (particularly the latter) to appear on screen in exactly the form it was first devised. All kinds of factors now enter into the equation. Discussions with the editor or producer will bring new thoughts, new strands to the plot, changed concepts of characters. The casting may be crucial. A small character may be played by an artiste who gives it a quality you had not even visualized at format stage, and it will rapidly become obvious you can afford to give that character more screen time. After the first episode appears on air, the public will take to some characters, dislike others and you will find yourself adjusting the later episodes accordingly. Perhaps the classic example of a Series changing shape was *The Avengers.* The first 13 episodes were a fairly straight down the line story about two men, played by Patrick McNee and Ian Hendry, in pursuit of private vengeance. The public took to the character played by McNee, who then began to form his dandy image. A new producer, John Bryce — a man of wild and antic imagination — then came on the scene. By sheer chance he was teamed up with Richard Bates, whose inventive mind matched his own. From this point on, writers contributing to the Series realized they were working with a creative team where literally any idea would not be considered too outrageous. The Series was starting to take off. The character of Emma Peel was not actually introduced until later on by a writer called Doreen Montgomery, who came in for a brief period as the story editor. The 'kinky leather' image was more or less an accident — the wardrobe people wanting to show what they could do. Since *The Avengers* has become something of a legend in television drama history, all kinds of people have claimed that they were the originators. But there was no one person, it just grew out of the separate talents of several people pooling their ideas at a time when there was a rush of new young talent in the industry and in a Television Company that encouraged experiment. (The only company, incidentally, that has ever been run by a writer — Howard Thomas.) The later, filmed version merely continued with a form that had already reached its peak of evolvement on videotape in studio.

Few Series or Serials have changed their shape so dramatically, but most of them will change to some degree. But sometimes they can change for the worse, particularly where there is a weak producer who lets the cast take over. Though I share the view of most writers that actors and actresses are the salt of the earth and have the deepest respect not simply for their talents, but for their sheer vitality and infinite goodness, few artistes can ever see a drama as a whole. Letting them loose on a script without tight directorial control is like giving a ball of wool to a litter of kittens. The writer must *always* be in control, even when he changes his mind. That is what is expected of him, not least by the cast.

The Spin-Off

All series and serials get old and tired. But sometimes a character or pair of characters have emerged so strongly as to create a positive public demand for them to continue. This happened with *Z-Cars* which spun-off into *Softly Softly*. This is not really something the new writer has to concern himself with at this stage — he will consider himself very lucky if he can even get the first series off the ground — but it can be a lucrative future to look forward to. Series and Serials, being of biological

65

construction, can breed, if only, like Cronos, by parturition from their own bone structure.

Adaptations and Dramatizations

The two are different, and we can deal with the first summarily. An *Adaptation* is the transference of a work already in dramatic form (e.g. a stage play) to another, television. It used to happen quite a lot in the early days when there was very little original material around and a lot of producers had come into television directly from the stage. But it is fairly rare today, and when it occurs, it is invariably handled by very experienced playwrights. Shaw plays appear from time to time, and of course, Shakespeare, but although Shakespeare plays are sometimes subtly abridged to fit a time slot, this can scarcely be called an adaptation, it is simply editing.

A *dramatization* is the term used for changing a prose work into a dramatic, dialogue version. There have been a vast range of classic novels dramatized for the box and some companies are now getting a bit desperate since they have used most of them up. Neither are we the only country doing it. The Germans are steadily ploughing through their entire literary output since the Middle Ages, so are the French, the Italians and increasingly, the Americans (though they have a more limited canvas).

It is extremely unlikely that a brand new writer will be given a dramatization to handle. It is a highly-skilled craft, and usually reserved for known professionals. Actually it is not always as difficult as everyone likes to pretend — it depends on the novel itself. Period novels from the eighteenth or nineteenth centuries, with their vast canvases, are certainly a bitch to handle, but increasingly the modern novel is being written — consciously or unconsciously — with the thought of a screen dramatization in the novelist's mind. A limited range of characters, confined settings, linear narrative and often huge chunks of dialogue mean that the job is half done. But just as dramatists seldom write clear prose, few novelists write 'actable' dialogue, so that is usually changed in any case.

If you have a favourite novel that you have always wanted to adapt, or maybe one of your own, there is no reason why you shouldn't put it up with a clear outline of how you would like to handle it. You just may be lucky.

The short story seldom adapts well, as it is either on a dying fall from the outset or relies entirely on a twist ending. Most viewers aren't prepared to sit around waiting for the twist, though Roald Dahl's *Tales of the Unexpected* was the exception to the rule. There is, of course that strange animal called the *Novella*, which is neither long enough to be called a novel nor short enough to be a long short story. Perhaps the classic case of the novella being brought triumphantly to the screen was *They Don't Shoot Horses, Do They?*, but that was originally written as a screenplay treatment, published as a novella when the Hollywood studios turned it down, they snapped up again when they found the book was a best seller.

If you *do* decide to attempt a dramatization, don't expect to manage it in one go. The literary texture of the book clings on persistently and the dramatist is reluctant at first to lose smaller characters or reconstruct plot in natural deference to the original author. Until you are confident enough to be ruthless, you will have to go through two stages — the first, a rough reconstruction, then, moving right away from the book which you now know by heart, approaching it as a straight piece of television drama.

Dramatizing popular thrillers can also be a lot more difficult than it seems at the outset. Many thriller writers spend a substantial part of the book building up atmosphere through description and laying little fragments of plot all over the place, then, right in the last chapter, there is a densely-packed chapter where all the loose ends tie up. In fact, the whole book has been building slowly to this climax. This structure works reasonably well if you are turning it into a feature film. The director can enjoy himself building up atmosphere because he has plenty of outside filming to play with; in any case, the audience is trapped in the cinema so can be kept waiting for the *dénouement*. But if you are trying to turn the same thriller into a six-parter for studio production, that structure doesn't work. You have to grab the audience with a climax and plenty of action from episode one, and you certainly can't spend the whole of episode six unravelling plot which depended for its comprehension on something that happened on screen six weeks prior, because by this time the viewer has forgotten what it was all about. So the thriller has to be completely reconstructed, with much of the plot moved back into earlier episodes. Ideally, you should have unravelled most of this by the time you get to the end of episode five, so leaving the final episode for fast action and the unravelling of the final strand. You will also find that quite often even the best selling thriller writers can be extraordinarily careless over plotting — relying on their style to paper over the cracks. But the television cameras scrutinize every detail and inconsistencies either of character or of plot will stick out like a sore thumb.

Viewers often complain that books translated into television drama have been changed, and regret the loss of their best-loved passages, but many of these remembered passages were purely descriptive, and where they may have utilized two or three thousand words in the book version, will be conveyed by the camera in a 30 second take — if the budget will stand the film sequence in the first place. Something has to fill that gap and it is up to the dramatist to reconstruct the plot accordingly.

Costume drama

With the invention of the colour video camera, costume drama really came into its own. Most of it falls under the Serial dramatization category already mentioned, but there is a certain amount of original material commissioned, particularly for children's programmes. This inevitably involves the writer in research and certain dangers ensue. It is very easy to fall in love with the research material and never get round to writing the script. Somehow you have to discipline yourself to select the essentials and ignore the rest. If you happen to enjoy reading history, and most writers do, there is nothing more relaxing than wandering down all kinds of delightful blind alleys. As in all research, whether for the screen or the novel, you have to develop the practice of scanning a tremendous amount of material very rapidly, steadfastly ignoring the irrelevant and, above all, knowing when to stop. You will also have to create period dialogue and that is not always what it seems. The novelists of the period are seldom much help — at least not those writing prior to the early part of the nineteenth century. They used a literary style — that, after all was what writing was, a stylish occupation. But it is often a poor guide to everyday spoken dialogue. You will have to create that yourself and in such a way that it does not sound either anachronistic or contrived. One of the most irritating criticisms writers of period dialogue have to face is that they are often accused of inserting Americanisms into late seventeenth or eighteenth century dialogue. In fact, many modern American words or phrases which sound particularly un-English are perfectly accurate for this period. They were taken over by the Pilgrim Fathers or the immigrants that followed over the next 100 years and have remained in American speech to this day — after they have fallen out of use in Britain.

But the process by which you create period characters is essentially no different from creating contemporary characters. The writer must forget the recorded literary style of the period and think himself into the minds of people living in that time, under those circumstances. One of the cherished illusions preserved by historians is that the English have always been a phlegmatic, unemotional race. I am indebted to John Prebble for once pointing out to me that, in the eighteenth century, the French regarded the English as a sloppy, sentimental race who were always bursting into tears.

Comedy

Comedy writers get paid almost twice as much as drama writers, but before you all rush to the joke book, there is a very sound reason for it. It is a bloody sight harder. Quite a few comedy writers work in pairs, not just to test each other's funny lines but quite often just to lift each other out of the state of depression that so often attends the practice of this sad craft. All comedy is a matter of careful timing. That is hard enough to judge in the theatre, where you can actually measure the time it takes for an audience first to absorb, then to respond to the joke. When you write for television there is no audience in sight. You are writing stone cold — what's more, your audience is in millions, not hundreds. A line that may cause a gentle rumbling of pleasure in Basingstoke will hit Wigan like a dead haddock. The subtle quip aimed at sophisticated Hampstead isn't going to sound all that hilarious in the Heart of Midlothian. The most common mistake that would-be comedy writers make (assuming they are genuinely funny in the first place) is putting the laugh lines too close together. A joke needs space either side of it in order that it can be both prepared for and reacted to. Small gags have to build up to bigger gags, as every practising comedian knows.

If you watch an Alan Ayckbourn comedy you will notice how often he builds his laughs in three stages — the first laugh line puts the audience in a state of expectation for the second, which draws the bigger laugh, then there is a perceptible gap before the third laugh line which invariably brings the house down *because it has been built for.* In comedy, no advice is sounder than the old tenet — tell them what you're going to do, do it, then tell them what you've done.

But the careful construction of laugh lines, important as it is as a technique, is not the first essential of comedy writing. The root of successful comedy is exactly the same as it is in drama, the creation of accurately observed characters and the placing of those characters in conflict. The main difference with comedy is that you have to do this *instantly,* the moment those characters appear in camera.

I mentioned earlier in this book that television comedy appears to be changing course, or more accurately, returning to certain Chekovian principles, laughter emerging from a contrasting sadness. Whether this is just a passing phase and television will soon fall back again on the faithful old formula of tits and bums, funny foreigners and heavy camp remains to be seen. There is certainly a great demand for good comedy at the moment. For many years the BBC held the lead, with the commercial companies trailing some distance behind. Recent offerings seem to suggest that the ITA stations have not simply caught up, but are actually forging ahead. It is certainly a highly competitive business with an equally high failure rate. You enter this game at your peril.

The half-hour sitcom will always be the staple diet, but not the only outlet. Most companies like to leaven their single play output with 50-minute comedies from time to time, and some drama serials contain a greater or lesser comedy element. There are single sketches for Light Entertainment shows and it is rumoured that not *all* the sketch material for satire shows *has* to come from ex-members of the Cambridge Footlights. The field is still relatively wide open and as I mentioned earlier, you can often say things in comedy that would cause a mild heart attack in drama departments.

Chapter Eleven

Dressing Up the Script . . .

> All that glisters is not gold

There is a perverse rule of thumb amongst editors and producers in British Television that the more impeccably the script is presented, the duller the contents. Part of the thinking behind this lies in our deep national affection for amateurism and its corollary, that true genius has a scruffy look, but oddly enough, it is often true. Tidy people often have untidy minds, and untidy people, tidy and disciplined minds. Some of the best writers in the business work from desks that look like compost heaps, though this is not an imperative for talent. I can only say from experience that if I receive a script in a beautifully manicured folder and accompanied by a letterhead printed in burnt sepia and its contents typed on an IBM golfball, my heart sinks.

But scripts are meant to be read by a number of people who don't have the time or patience to decipher a badly-typed script full of unintelligible hand written amendments.

Sending in the fourth copy isn't likely to get a very favourable response either. The producer knows that the script has already been the rounds and the top copy is lying in some other company's drawer. It is a second hand offering. The most acceptable layout is the one I used on page 35 for the Jack and Jill example. Dialogue is normally down the right hand side of the page, thus:

1. INT. RUPERT'S STUDY. STUDIO. DAY.   1.

RUPERT IS AT HIS DESK, HIS HEAD IN HIS HANDS. HE IS WEEPING. THE DOOR OPENS AND A YOUNG MAN ENTERS. HE IS WEARING A MONTAGU BURTON SUIT AND CARRIES A BLACK LEATHER BRIEFCASE IN ONE HAND, A KNOUT IN THE OTHER. HIS NAME IS ARTHUR.

> ARTHUR: Hullo, I'm your friendly neighbourhood
> VAT Inspector.

RUPERT JUMPS UP FROM HIS SEAT LIKE A SCALDED CAT AND LEAPS

OUT OF THE WINDOW. This is the normal layout for studio tape production. The margin on the left hand side is for the editor or producer to make rude remarks and the director to rough in his camera directions.

For some reason, lost in the mists of time, the layout for film and its offspring, the television film is arranged differently:—

1.   EXT. BUSY STREET. DAY.   1.
_____

RUPERT is running down the street as fast as he can, ARTHUR in pursuit.
RUPERT rushes across the road, narrowly avoiding a DOUBLE DECKER BUS.
ARTHUR shouts after the retreating figure.
                              ARTHUR:
               Come back! You're entitled to a rebate.
CUT TO RUPERT. He stops, turns. C.U. his face showing intense relief.
He waits for ARTHUR to catch up with him.
                              RUPERT:
               Oh hullo. I was just off to post a letter.
RUPERT and ARTHUR return to RUPERT'S HOUSE arm in arm.

Nothing very difficult about either layout, and if you get it wrong, no-one will bother very much.

This is the *draft script* and if you are very lucky it will be the final script, but usually there will be amendments and changes.

On the front page you should list the characters, sets and any outside filming needed.

Once accepted, this will be typed up again and duplicated for the *Rehearsal Script,* more or less the same as your own script but with certain information added, like the rehearsal dates, production staff, outside filming dates, etc. From this, the Director will have prepared his *Camera Script* with all the camera moves and angles listed, but this is not your concern.

If the new writer gets that far, the rest is plain sailing. You will learn as you go along. But the question most new writers want to know is how you get to that stage in the first place.

Should I send the script direct, or must I have an agent?

All the companies, and of course, the BBC, have script departments. Some are more efficient than others, but they are the proper people to send unsolicited scripts to, so use them. Don't send scripts directly to producers unless you know them personally. The script will just lie around in his drawer. And *never* send scripts to actors. You will be extremely lucky if it is ever returned and actors really don't have much pull inside television as far as scripts are concerned.

Yes, you will almost certainly need an agent, but most of the leading writers' agencies already have very full lists, so it is not always easy to find one who will take you on. You stand a much better chance if you have already had something put on somewhere, if only at a fringe theatre. A lot of new writers sell their first script direct, then go to an agent to handle them from there on. But you should try. That is what agents are for, and since the mortality rate amongst television writers is fairly high, there may be a space on his list.

But don't expect too much from agents. The best ones certainly know what is going on in the industry and have frequent lunches with buyers where they have the opportunity to push their clients. On the other hand, it isn't always easy to push a new writer with no track record. As far as the negotiation of fees is concerned, it is useful to have someone to do it for you, but not essential. Fee structures in television have been laid down over the years by negotiation between the BBC, the ITA companies and the Writers Guild and these have tended to become the norm. A tough agent may be able to negotiate a few hundred pounds above what is termed the 'going rate', but since most of this will be swallowed up by the agency fee, there isn't a great deal in it. Agency fees are a standard ten per cent of the fee. Never go on the books of any agent who tries to charge you more — he will almost certainly be a fly-by-night who will have no standing or pull with the companies anyway.

There is also a highly complex scale of overseas royalties and repeat fees, sometimes they can add substantially to your income. These too are all codified in the relevant Guild agreements. You should, by the way, join the Guild as soon as you have had something produced. Although it now has permanent staff, it was formed and is governed by professional writers who give their services free. It has a pension plan and now runs a collecting agency jointly with the Society of Authors. Quite apart from the direct benefits in ensuring that contracts are strictly adhered to, it campaigns ceaselessly for the improvement of the writer's status in the industry. It is also the only opportunity you will have of meeting other writers and exchanging experiences. Writing is a lonely job and some social contact between writers can do a lot to lift your spirits.

Chapter Twelve

The Television Writer . . .

What *is* he?

Firstly, let me apologize for the constant use throughout this book of masculine gender. It is simply a matter of convenience. 'He/She' looks clumsy. Some may argue that I might equally have used 'She' throughout, and there is really no answer to that. It is simply a matter of convention. But let it be said quite clearly that there is no differentiation whatever between male and female writers in the industry. Each gender has excelled, and amongst writers themselves there are no patronizing attitudes (or none that I have detected, women may say differently). Personally, I marginally prefer to work with women producers as they waste less time in small talk and usually have a clearer idea of what they are looking for, but whether women writers have the same reaction, I wouldn't know.

But there has often been a tendency for companies to engage women writers exclusively for what are called 'women's subjects'. Unless you are writing about childbirth there isn't a great deal of logic in this; a writer is a writer and should be able to write for both sexes. If he, or she can't, then they have not fully learnt their trade.

You may also notice that nowhere (until now) have I used the term 'scriptwriter'. I have always found this term vaguely insulting, used as a denial of authorship — and certainly it is often used in the Press as a form of derogation. This is not just a petty cavil, but a matter of self respect. While Blacks allowed themselves to be called niggers and coons, they accepted that role and kow-towed accordingly. The same is true of writers. If you are engaged in writing drama or comedy — whether in pure original form or as dramatizers of prose works, you are a playwright, dramatist or comedy writer. So long as writers accept terms that diminish their roles, they will continue to hide behind these terms and use it as an excuse for the failure to take full responsibility for their work.

Neither should you use a pseudonym in television, and very few writers do. The use of a pseudonym is another way of saying you are not proud of your work and want to play 'shrinking violet'. There is only one exception. If the Corporation or company has so bowdlerized your work that you are ashamed of it, then there is a positive duty to take your name off it. There is nothing more galling than being slated by the Press for work which now bears little resemblance to the script you first submitted.

Typecasting is another serious problem for television writers, just as it is for actors. A writer who allows himself to get bogged down in a long running serial will, for ever after be known amongst script departments as a soap opera hack. He may have to switch media altogether to change that image — perhaps with a stage play or by writing a novel. In fact, the problems of *surviving* in the industry are as great, if not greater than breaking in in the first place. The writer must always be on his toes, spreading the work between channels, avoiding labels, and hardest of all, keeping fresh.

Role Playing

In the professional life of a television writer he may play many roles, and may be seen from many different aspects. Let us examine a few of them:

Writer as creator

That is the image every new writer has of himself, and many hardbitten old hands still preserve in a special compartment in their minds. The man of ideas, the fountain of invention — constantly throwing out new thoughts, new angles on old conventions, dazzling producers with his inventive imagination. That is the life of bliss, and any writer who can maintain this role through thick and thin, periods of elation and depression, will die a happy man.

Writer as hack

The time server, the company man, the writer who can be totally relied upon to produce the goods to fit the market. He is the faithful old standby whom a producer can always turn to when he is in trouble and a script is needed in 14 days flat to fill a hole in the schedule. Curiously enough, he is seldom doing it for the money, his achilles heel is *flattery*. 'Only *you*,' the producer will say to him, 'can help us in our hour of need.' And off he will go back to his typewriter, burning the midnight oil on subjects which don't excite him in the least except as a challenge to his professional skill. He, too, can die a happy man so long as he never stops to examine what is happening to him.

Writer as highly paid whore

Not to be confused with the above. The hack may never know he is hacking, the writer-whore not only *knows* he is whoring, but *why*. Like all the best streetwalkers, he is only doing it to put his little golden-haired daughter through convent school. He knows he is capable of real love, pure thought, but keeps that capacity locked away where none of his regular clients can reach it. While he is whoring away with the best of them, he knows he is capable of finer things — the ones he *really* wants to write. Sadly, he seldom gets round to writing them.

Writer as shrinking violet

Most writers, however experienced, go through periods when they are deeply uncertain of their own talent, or, more often, that they have not achieved what they set out to achieve. In a brash industry like television, where salesmanship is a vital ingredient of the production process, you will often find yourself faced with a battery of people, from producers to directors, who appear supremely self confident in their opinions. It is very easy to find yourself crushed and intimidated by their demands.

It is only the most talented directors who feel sufficiently certain of their own talent to express self doubt, but the new writer will be lucky to find one of those. Different writers react to the situation in different ways. Some develop a surface arrogance to mask their fears, but it is often a very transparent pose. Others — male and female, assume an old fashioned feminine role.

'I am just a poor little writer,' they are saying in effect, 'slaving at home over a hot typewriter with only my fragile talent to offer.'

These are the shrinking violets, and unless they can play the game with supreme feminine guile — Josephine to the director's Napoleon, they are a positive menace, both to themselves and everyone they work with. All too often they will yield too easily in the early stages of production, then, when they see the adulterated product on screen, protest far too late that they have been robbed.

In the febrile world of broadcasting, creative doubts are inevitable, but modesty is no virtue.

Writer as guru

At whatever level the writer finds himself, he will be expected to be just slightly wiser and cleverer than the company he keeps. That, after all, is what he was engaged for. Some writers find it useful to cultivate that image. They may not always have a string of polished epigrams to hand, but a brooding silence can be just as effective. (Beware, I once held a brooding silence at a script conference for so long that I fell asleep.)

The guru writer will never explain too much, but throw out the odd fragmented image and leave the ends of his sentences in the air. The guru director will often use the same technique and the two of them discussing a scene together is final proof that telepathy not only exists, but is common form of communication inside television.

'What we need here is a kind of . . .'
'Right . . .'
'Are you with me?'
'Absolutely . . . but supposing I . . .?'
'So long as you don't . . .'
'Oh, Christ, no. That would ruin the whole concept.'

Writer as Radical Reformer

Most writers in television are on the side of the reforming angels, but don't necessarily fit into popular ideological groups. Because they are accustomed to presenting both sides of any conflict, they can usually hold totally opposing viewpoints in balance without any outward signs of strain.

The position of the freelance writer in society is a peculiar one. In his lifestyle he is the epitome of what the extreme Right Wing monetarist would regard as the perfect citizen. He lives by what he can sell in the open market against keen competition. Copyright is, by definition, a property right (on the Continent it is grandly called an intellectual property). Since his profession is not recognized as a form of employment, he cannot even draw unemployment benefit when he is out of work. He will never draw redundancy money when the television stations start making economy cuts because he was never on their books in the first place. Even the most overtly Left Wing writer will feel secretly proud of this status while roundly condemning it as a way of life for others. A Right Wing writer (and there are quite a few in television despite the popular myth that it is all in the hands of Leftist trendies), will have separate compartments in his mind for liberal causes. This is why writers are regarded with suspicion by most governments throughout the world. They cannot be trusted to be consistent. According to Amnesty International, there are now *seventy* member states of the United Nations holding political prisoners — a substantial number of them are writers. In the West there is no need to lock them up, the communications industry is such a Tower of Babel, few can hear their voices above the clamour.

They are almost the last of the independent craftsmen to survive the industrial revolution — along with potters and violin makers. With luck and stubborn persistence, they may just last out until the next Renaissance. If they don't, there won't be a Renaissance.

The writer is also a small businessman, a sub-contractor and occasionally, if he makes enough money to meet serious tax problems, a director of his own company.

Finally, a writer is only a writer when he is engaged at it full-time and has no other source of income. A part-timer, clinging on to the security of his job while trying to write in his spare time is like a swimmer with one hand on the side of the bath. When you take that decision to become a writer, you must plunge in at the deep end, and be prepared to drown.

What Next?

For the twenty-five years I have worked inside television as a general writing practitioner, the industry has maintained the same basic structure. Although there have been significant technical developments — from 'live' to tape, from monochrome to colour — it has always been a form of visual *broadcasting*. With an open-handed generosity unusual for our commercial age, an endless stream of entertainment, from comedy and drama to sport, documentary feature to in-depth news has been poured into millions of homes for the nominal payment of a small licence fee. Fortunes have been made, principally by the commercial stations, but not least by the manufacturers of television sets and their ancillary equipment. Because the system provided a 'licence to print money', in Lord Thompson's unforgettable phrase, no-one really bothered to think about how absurdly cheap it was to the consumer compared with other products. The average householder pays twice as much for his water — which falls freely from the Heavens — than for 300 hours of entertainment a week spread across four channels.

It has been obvious for some time that this state of affairs would not continue for ever, but any fundamental change in the market had to await new technology; alternate means of conveying the product to the consumer under controlled conditions. From the moment the videotape recorder was invented, it became clear that the equipment was available to bring about that change. The video replay cassette was the worm in the bud of the concept of open broadcasting. It was just a question of how soon it could be made sufficiently compact and produced cheaply enough to make it a viable proposition on the market. That time has now come, and the domestic VTR recorder is shortly to be succeeded by the videodisc — which has the added advantage to the producing organizations that it cannot be used for piracy since it has no recording facility. Hard on the heels of the expanding video recorder market, we are now promised two Direct Broadcast Satellites, to be allocated to the BBC and up to thirty cable channels before the end of the decade. Whether there will be sufficient material to supply all these multiple outlets is a matter of some speculation.

The present networks, both BBC and the IBA stations have expressed the fear that the arrival of 'narrowcasting', will mean the writing on the wall for open air broadcasting, denuding the existing channels of the best material to feed the more lucrative cable stations. In the United States this is already beginning to happen, and the networks are rapidly re-investing their capital in cable. But there is already a feeling that with all these additional entertainment outlets, the public may be putting up consumer resistance.

There must be a saturation point, so forecasting the state of the entertainments industry of the future is a hazardous business. But the fragmentation of the old system of centrally transmitted, low cost to the consumer programming now seems irreversable. Television will begin to look more like the publishing industry, with different sections of the market being supplied with more specialised programming according to taste, cost and demand. The only thing we need be concerned with here is the possible effect on writers for the medium.

On the face of it, opportunities for writers should increase. Channel 4, with its statutory duty to engage independent producers already appears to be responsible for a limited revival of the British film industry. The cable stations will need feeding with new material. The videocasette and video disc retailers are already running out of old films and calling for new products. So, assuming the public have the cash to pay for it — and that is an open question — the demand for writers and writing must increase. But the pattern will almost certainly change. Writers may no longer command audiences of millions, except for high budget films capable of being exploited through multiple outlets. It will be altogether a more risky business with a far higher casualty rate. Writers need have no fear of that, they are in a catch as catch can profession.

Chapter Thirteen

The Creative Process . . .

But there are some things that will never change, the *fundamental creative process* by which a certain number of individuals in every society elect to distill images from their surroundings and construct them into a narrative for the entertainment or enlightenment of the rest. These are the writers, and this book set out to explain *some* of the methods by which they do so through the television screen. I am deeply conscious that there is still a great deal left unsaid; that some of the things I have written would be challenged by my colleagues, who have evolved their own systems and view the medium in a different light. I was aware from the outset that many professionals will see the title of this book as misleading or pretentious. There is no single *Way to Write*. If these words are to be taken at their surface meaning, they are certainly making too bold a claim. But if the phrase *The Way To* can be taken to mean *The Route Towards*. . . . then the ambivalence in the title may be amply justified.

There are statements in this book with which the buyers of television scripts may disagree, even take exception to. They issue their own advice to writers and consider it reasonably close to Gospel. But television companies do not *see themselves* as writers see them. This is particularly true of the upper echelons of management, to whom writers are often seen as remote figures, necessary but rather ungrateful to their sponsors. Curiously enough, the biggest gap in understanding does not lie with the commercial stations, who tend to regard the relationship between writers and themselves as a straightforward trading deal, but with the BBC.

Writing for the Corporation has many advantages: it is huge, it has a wide range of back-up facilities, it contains civilized and sensitive people at production level (as do many of the commercial companies), but it is obsessed with its role as *patron* of the arts. Senior management and Boards of Governors tend to see themselves as latter day Florentine Medicis, promoters and guardians of all that is best in modern culture, offering stimulating opportunities to the craftsmen and apprentices under their benevolent rule.

81

The modern television writer hates patronage. He regards the BBC as his publisher, not his patron. He sees no reason for displaying gratitude for performing a function without which the Medicis of Shepherds Bush would have no justification for existence, except as a news and sports channel.

The readers of this book, most of whom have as yet had no direct experience of the Corporation or the companies, apart from polite rejection slips, may feel that this is of only academic interest; the sour meanderings of an old pro trying to score points off adversaries. But the way in which a writer sees both his role and the role of those he hopes to work with *is* important because it will affect his attitude to his own work. That is why I have tried to paint a picture of the television writer in the context of his work, rather than make this book a simple training manual.

> *It is of vital importance for the future of the television industry that the writer shall retain his independence of spirit, entering the industry as a free man who owes nothing to anyone but himself and his audience.*

Without that determination, the creative process, however fertile in the beginning, will eventually be aborted.

The Arvon Experience . . .

Practically all large industries have their training schemes, their laboratories or workshops where the novice can learn his trade. Television has no laboratories or workshops for writers. No closed circuit studios where the new writer may experiment and learn the rudiments of writing for the visual medium and the sophisticated techniques of production. It is an extraordinary omission for an industry of this size. It can only be explained by the belief that writers are born, not made. It seems to be of little concern to the companies that many writers are born to blush unseen or wither unheard of. Companies have script and story editors, of course, whose job it is supposed to be to cultivate the new writer. But most editors are under considerable production pressure and have little time or patience to teach the rudiments of the craft. Many could not do so if they were given the opportunity, not all editors are writers and to those who are, the question must always be asked — why aren't you writing instead of editing?

It has taken two poets, John Moat and John Fairfax, creators of the Arvon Foundation, to fulfil a responsibility that the television companies, for all their power and wealth, have failed to assume. They have established a creative workshop where the new writer, whether for poetry, the novel or television (and the three are, or should be, much closer interwoven than might first appear) can work alongside the practitioner in an atmosphere free from commercial pressures.

However cynical we become in later life, about product, about markets, about money and merchandise, there is still something exciting and stimulating in the creative experience *as an experience in itself*. By some peculiar chemistry, which I would not even attempt to define, Arvon allows that experience to take place in an atmosphere of honesty and trust.

Although I began by calling the television writer the invisible factor in production, the extent to which writers for the greatest stage in history are prepared to remain invisible depends largely on the writers of the future, how confident they are, how determined to establish their own individual imprint. Much of that confidence comes with practice, but it springs from a single, unique experience — the discovery in themselves of the creative impulse. That is not something that can be acquired, rather is it something that must be uncovered. It was there in childhood, when all experience was new and you approached the world with a sense of wonder.

Freud, although he claimed that he did not understand the creative writing process and regarded it with envy, nevertheless came nearest to finding the key.

> Might we not say that every child at play behaves like a creative writer, in that he creates a world of his own, or rather, rearranges the things of his world in a new way that pleases him?
>
> Sigmund Freud. *Creative writers and daydreaming.*

pragmatic - officials, dogmatic